LIVING WITH INDIFFERENCE

Studies in Continental Thought

John Sallis, general editor

Living with Indifference

CHARLES E. SCOTT

Indiana University Press
Bloomington & Indianapolis

"The Academy of Fine Ideas" is from *The Collected Poems of Wallace Stevens* by Wallace Stevens, copyright 1954 by Wallace Stevens and renewed 1982 by Holly Stevens. Used by permission of Alfred A. Knopf, a division of Random House, Inc. "Apology for Bad Dreams" is from *Selected Poetry of Robinson Jeffers* by Robinson Jeffers, copyright 1925 and renewed 1953 by Robinson Jeffers. Used by permission of Random House, Inc. "what Got him Noth" is from *Complete Poems: 1904–1962* by E. E. Cummings, edited by George J. Firmage, copyright 1957, 1985, 1991 by the Trustees for the E. E. Cummings Trust. Used by permission of Liveright Publishing Corporation.

This book is a publication of

Indiana University Press
601 North Morton Street
Bloomington, IN 47404-3797 USA

http://iupress.indiana.edu

Telephone orders   800-842-6796
Fax orders   812-855-7931
Orders by e-mail   iuporder@indiana.edu

The paper used in this publication meets the minimum requirements of American National Standard for Information Sciences—Permanence of Paper for Printed Library Materials, ANSI Z39.48-1984.

MANUFACTURED IN THE UNITED STATES OF AMERICA

Library of Congress Cataloging-in-Publication Data

Scott, Charles E.
  Living with indifference / Charles E. Scott.
      p. cm. — (Studies in continental thought)
  Includes index.
  ISBN 978-0-253-34856-2 (cloth : alk. paper) — ISBN 978-0-253-21900-8 (pbk. : alk. paper) 1. Indifferentism (Ethics) 2. Apathy. I. Title.
  BJ1535.I63S36 2007
  170—dc22
                                           2006029097

1 2 3 4 5   12 11 10 09 08 07

For Vincent Colapietro, John Sallis,
Dennis Schmidt, John Stuhr,
and Nancy Tuana

CONTENTS

ACKNOWLEDGMENTS

Special thanks to Charlie and Sue Ruffing, Glenn Gustafson, Kathy and Dennis Haggarty, Stephen Miller, Stephen Swoyer, and Charles R. Scott for technological help at times that seemed like crises in their moments. During the several years of conception and writing I received valuable assistance from Juliana Eimer, Bryan Lueck, Omar Rivera, and Henry Wang. Many friends and critics responded to chapters and parts of chapters with helpful comments. Penn State University and especially Susan Welch, dean of the College of Liberal Arts, provided important and appreciated support. Susan Schoenbohm made the difference that turns assistance and insight into a work considerably exceeding kindness. Vincent Colapietro, John Sallis, Dennis Schmidt, John Stuhr, and Nancy Tuana provided incomparable collegiality and good counsel, transforming what Stevens might call the assassin's song into occasions of friendship.

LIVING WITH INDIFFERENCE

ONE

Speaking of Indifference

If men were able to exercise complete control over their
circumstances . . . they would never be prey to superstition.
—Spinoza

Philosophy is a matter of texts, of texts that began the problems and ideas of a tradition, of texts that changed the course of traditions or deepened and widened them, of texts that turned away from traditions in the impact of new problems and ways of thinking. That, however, is only part of philosophy's story, because it also arises out of and reflects the texture of people's experiences, the vast and intricate intuitive network of symbols, practices, and manners of feeling that give experience its intensities, rhythms, kinships, and differences. Texts are only a part of philosophy's fertile ground, and we would limit unwisely the discipline and passion of philosophy were we to restrict it to texts.

Without texts, on the other hand, we would lose touch with lineages of reflective formulation and determination. They provide centers of perspective and interest, molding and shaping the intuitive, experiential grounds, giving limited voice to all manner of observations and feelings. Texts give places of speech and teaching and control; they make possible disciplined orders. In this remarkable strength we find also the vulnerability of texts: In their orders and disciplined networks of careful articulation they make evident the chaotic differences of experiences—the differences that limit and exceed philosophy's care, order, and language—streams of experience entirely different from philosophical virtues, mute where order and good sense prevail, merely neutral before the great figurations of ideas, beliefs, and value: dimensions of indifference in human experience in which philosophy ceases. And not only philosophy ceases. What we in the West broadly think of as humanity ceases, human control and influence cease in the dimension of indifference that accompanies all human engagements. I expect that all philosophical texts in the Western traditions carry a more or less muted sense of something like a region of indifference in their determinations and regulations. Scarcely marked, it hovers in thought on time, chance, beauty, imagination, freedom, violence, and virtue. I will note many of those texts and thoughts as I address the indifferent dimension in our lives. I will also turn to manners of expression that in their deviation from philosophical order find access to indifference that most disciplined philosophy ignores and does not see.

This book is about the dimension of indifference that appears with emphasis in experiences of beauty, contemplation, transformation, dissolution, inevitability, objectivity, and, I shall say, most markedly in experiences of freedom and goodness.

How might we speak of indifference? In the context of a book, that is partially a question of texture. Does the topic require a weave of interconnections that forms a unity of regulated interacting concepts, a unified whole? That kind of system would make a self-standing construct, an individualized and identifiable entity. What if indifference were not a self-standing entity? Wouldn't the texture of such a book mislead and at best present badly its subject matter? And if I intend to speak of a dimension of living things—in this case, a dimension of indifference—and not speak of something called indifference itself, wouldn't a definitive and differentiated position that shows no indifference be an embarrassment? Something like missing the point?

If there were a point. Indifference is not something with a point. It doesn't take place like a culmination of many things. The problem is that the happening of sheer neutrality is not a thing at all. "It" lacks specific determination, and that makes thinking and speaking of indifference awkward. My guess is that the most appropriate address of indifference is indirect and that directness regarding indifference is at best preparatory for another kind of perceptiveness.

The texture for this address needs to function like a wave-link attuned to an indifferent frequency. It needs to develop a resonance with the persistent unraveling of orders, with an unruly dimension in living that seems apparent in the permeability of borders, that is like a space of differences, and that gives no order to simultaneous events in a regulatory Now.

So if I am to make a systematic presentation of indifference I will need to find recurring and interacting issues and questions regarding the dimension of indifference. Those would help to constitute a texture and would be issues and questions that compose a linking resonance and hold off balance expectation for a completed whole as well as the implications of "a" and "the" when they modify "indifference," hold the pronoun "it" questionable in its application to indifference.

How could we formulate a resonance with indifference, since indifference lacks a fixed shape? The texture of this book has many representative statements, many values and perspectives expressed in it, but it does not find its subject matter in them or in a unitary force. If the book finds an equilibrium, it will not be in a group of dominant values or direct claims but in a poise that is unmoved by the several persistent elements that define the book's values and concepts, a poise by which space appears that is undefined by those values and concepts, a poise that is resonant with such space as it defines its own determinate shape. If the book succeeds, its texture will comprise that kind of equilibrium—a formulated and determined resonance with the dimension of indifference that is the book's subject matter, a dimension of indetermination that appears to accompany the determinations that define our lives and our world. It is a dimension that challenges discursive, performative adherence to it, "challenges" in the sense of "provokes and holds in question." It is especially provoking because regardless of the transitive verbs I just used, "it" doesn't do a thing. The book's texture does not adhere to indifference, but it does intend to find its "place" by maintaining attention to the indifference of its own space and occurrence without turning such space and occurrence into any thing that is identified or fixed.

Throughout the book I highlight several meanings for "indifferent." Its basic philosophical sense is "not different"—the prefix "in-" functions as a negation. Its pervasive sense of "undifferentiated" may be nuanced by an implication of neutrality and impartiality, by an absence of interest, care, or intention. It might describe a lack of connection or importance: an indifferent matter or quality, for example. It can suggest neutrality regarding good and evil, or lack of an active quality.

"Indifference" suggests more explicitly than "indifferent" a lack of feeling for or against anything: the vast indifference of the universe, for example. Or inertia where will is concerned, want of sufficient importance to constitute a difference—an indifferent presence—pervasive heedlessness, and, as noted above, lack of connection.

But the word, stemming as it does from difference and *differre*, also suggests possibility for change and movement toward unspecified differentiation. It suggests possible determination without partiality and with neutrality toward the outcome—quite different from teleological intentions. This sense of indifferent force as opening to determination will play an important role in the following chapters. In this context the book engages senses and concepts of necessity and chance, especially in relation to experiences of beauty and figurations of spirit. Experiences and concepts of limitation, probability, dispersion, inconstancy, and space also have their parts to play as we approach the indetermination of indifference. And throughout the book freedom and goodness will appear as axes in many human experiences in which dimensions of indifference make their appearance.

This book is not primarily about the attitudes of people, about whether they care passionately about values and lives. But it is nonetheless about attitudes, attitudes that form when people have a disturbing sense that something important is hidden from them. In such instances we might try to reproduce the hidden "reality"; but rather than finding the secret, we find the stock-in-trade images of our ordinary lives, shadowed still by something hidden, perhaps mysterious and seemingly important, and especially important if the hidden doesn't seem to be like a real thing with determined identity. Dimensions of indifference in many instances, given certain expectations about reality and mores based on those expectations, figure "something" hidden and important. The very happening of these dimensions threatens some large views of the world and often disturbs the hopes and comforts we take in situations of stress and pain. Patterns of denial can develop; for example, insistence on personalized and intentional universals that are free of indifference, teleological speculations about the world's continuity, and ethics of attachment. In such instances, indifference in the occurring of lives can become a negative preoccupation in the positive meanings of people's lives—like a dark specter of meaninglessness that requires well-tended vigilance at the deepest levels of affirmation and hope. Often in those situations one finds insistence on systematic tightness, emphasis on definitive closure, passions focused primarily by shared identity, and a dominance of values of conformity in conceptions of community and commonality.

I have seen the eyes of indifferent people, as I am sure you have. Their cold preoccupation, their blindness to compassion, their failure to notice or care. This book is not about them and is largely indifferent to them. It—the book—is rather about aspects of indifference in living events, not about a kind of character described as indifferent. It is about dimensions of occurrence that are utterly neutral and without intention. And it is also about some of the differences that paying attention to such dimensions makes. It is preoccupied by differences in sensibility that can arise when people are aware of dimensions of indifference throughout their lives, and, far from traumatized or obsessed by them, accept them and themselves with them, and develop, perhaps, values that take constructive account of those dimensions and the departures and beginnings that they occasion.

I turn now to a different texturing of this introductory chapter in anticipation of the chapters that follow. The purpose of this different form of presentation is to introduce both a sensibility that appears attuned to dimensions of indifference in living events and highly disciplined articulations of this sensibility.

Consider this statement by Jerry Fodor:

> It's very hard to get this right because of our penchant for teleology, for ex-
> plaining things on the model of agents with beliefs, goals, and desires is in-
> veterate and probably itself innate. We are forever wanting to know what
> things are for, and we don't like having to take Nothing for an answer. That
> gives us a wonderful head start on understanding the practical psychology of
> ourselves and our conspecifics; but it is not of the (no doubt many) respects
> in which we aren't kinds of creatures ideally equipped for doing natural sci-
> ence. Still I think that sometimes out of the corner of an eye, "at a moment
> which is not action or inaction," we can glimpse the true scientific fission:
> austere, tragic, alienated and very beautiful. A world that isn't for anything;
> a world that is just there.[1]

According to this observation, when people experience the world as
"just there," our penchant for explaining things on the model of active subjects will likely lose some effective force. Lost too, presumably, would be the
force in images of ourselves as *thoroughly* agential, *thoroughly* purposeful,
rightfully exercising dominion in the name of good and true purposes. In
the language of this book, things happen with a dimension of being good
for nothing. That's a dimension of their lives—of *our* lives. When we catch
a glimpse of moments "which [are] not action or inaction" we see another
possibility: life other to purpose and differential caring, indifferent life,
"austere, tragic, alienated, and very beautiful."

In a different idiom, e. e. cummings:

> what Got him was Noth
> ing & nothing's exact
> ly what any
> one Living(or some
> body Dead
> like even a Poet)could
> hardly express what
> I Mean is
> what knocked him over Wasn't

1. Jerry Fodor, *In Critical Condition* (Cambridge, Mass.: MIT Press, 1998), 16.

(for instance)the Knowing your
whole(yes god
damned)life is a Flop or even
to
Feel how
Everything(dreamed
& hoped &
prayed for
months & weeks & days & years
& nights &
forever)is Less than
Nothing(which would have been
Something)what got him was nothing[2]

Indifference "is" not a thing. That's one of the reasons why the question of the book's texture is hard for me because texture determines things in their weave. I'm addressing "not different" in the occurrences of differences, "not different without action or inaction," and addressing too a sense of indifference that is not at all foreign to Western judgment and sensibility and that often has functioned as though it were a secret or something threatening and effecting a destructive emphasis on subjectlike projection and control. Nothing especially mystical and nothing systematic, but *nothing* that gets to us, scares us, or shocks us (certainly doesn't humor us) and leaves us wanting to Do Something about the fragments, detachments, and chances of living. To cover over the spaces, as it were. To bring it to definitive expression. To exact it in a texture of images and discourse. And not, I suppose, to think it differently, holding firm as it were to its indetermination and giving the lie to what some people think of as mystical in the sense of "it doesn't fit our interpretation of 'intelligent.'"

In *The Book of Illusions* Paul Auster writes of silent films:

They were like poems, like the renderings of dreams, like some intricate choreography of the spirit, and because they were dead, they probably spoke more deeply to us now than they had to the audience of their time. We watched the same great chasm of forgetfulness, and the very things that separated them from us were in fact what made them so arresting: their muteness, their absence of color, their fitful, speeded-up rhythms. These were obstacles, and they made viewing difficult for us, but they also relieved the

2. e. e. cummings, *95 Poems* (New York: Harcourt, Brace, Jovanovich, 1958), 30.

images of the burden of representation. They stood between us and the film, and therefore we no longer had to pretend that we were looking at the real world.[3]

Relieving images of the burden of representation is hard, and I think a fundamental shift in sensibility and attitudes is often necessary for that relief to happen. Auster finds that what makes silent films arresting and allows them to speak deeply to us is what makes them difficult for us: their detachment from us, their muteness, their absence of color, and their fitful, speeded-up rhythms. These films are difficult in part because most of what we consider real in the world doesn't happen in them. The movements of the characters and animals, subtitles, the speed of transitions, the silence—not like the world really is. But in their illusory quality—illusory in comparison to the nonpoetic world—something else happens that is not subject to the staple of reality: representation. Auster doesn't say "bad representation." He says "not representable." Silent films open a dimension that seems illusory in our usual way of knowing things, and in this opening a sensibility begins to emerge that is not directly presentable. He writes from it and of it—not of angels or other figurations like that, but of an illusory, palpable aspect in the occurrence of things that makes the boundaries of ordinary clarity seem relative and limited, sometimes protective and overassured.

Much later in the book the narrator says:

> All I know is that I wasn't afraid. When Alma Grund pulled out that revolver and pointed it at my chest, it didn't strike fear in me so much as fascination. I understood that the bullets in the gun contained a thought that had never occurred to me before. The world was full of holes, tiny apertures of meaninglessness, microscopic rifts that the mind could walk through, and once you were on the other side of one of those holes, you were free of yourself, free of your life, free of your death, free of everything that belonged to you. I had chanced upon one of them in my living room that night. It appeared in the form of a gun, and now that I was inside that gun, I didn't care whether I got out or not. I was perfectly calm and perfectly insane, perfectly prepared to accept what the moment had offered. Indifference of that magnitude is rare, and because it can be achieved only by someone ready to let go of who he is, it demands respect. In inspires awe in those who gaze upon it.[4]

Auster is far from suggesting an attitude of indifference to death and self that forms a model for those of us who want to find the right approach to living. He is describing a situation in which, like in his experience of

---

3. Paul Auster, *Picador* (New York: Henry Holt, 2002), 15.
4. Auster, *Picador,* 109–10.

silent films, he is alert to a detached and nonrepresentable dimension of occurrence that is indifferent to meaning, particular lives, and the value of
being a self. "It" doesn't fit the texture of identifiable and disposable reality.
"It" doesn't do anything. His way of appropriating these "tiny apertures" is
particular to him and the moment of threat. He can speak of what is going
on—Alma Grund, the gun, the events that led up to the moment—but
even then, in the speaking, he is alert, not so much to the illusion of the
tiny apertures as to the illusory aspect in his realistic, descriptive speaking.
Are the little gaps there? Are they real? Does the image of tiny apertures represent something that is there? Not really. A sensibility is articulated that
does not look to resolve events exclusively into "real" and "imagined." Different sensibilities can have incommensurate alertness—a fundamentally
conservative Islamic sensibility, for example, and a liberal democratic one.
Those thoroughly different manners of experience and perception are not
exactly representable to each other, nor is what they directly know and embody directly representable. In Auster's articulation (and in cummings's as
well) such alertness would be carried out best by varieties of images, stories,
thoughts, perhaps by forms of self-correction, perhaps by collapses of meaning and reference—by that kind of texture and weave. And occasionally by
unresolved and contradictory claims—by concepts and images, for example, that are connected at times by dimensions of awareness in which detachment, incommensurability, and neither action nor nonaction happen:
alertness with indifference as well as with action, value, and intentional perspective.

Wallace Stevens writes:

> The law of chaos is the law of ideas,
> Of improvisations and seasons of belief.
> Ideas are of men, the mass of meaning and
> The mass of men are one. Chaos is not
> The mass of meaning. It is three or four
> Ideas or, say, five men or, possibly six.[5]

From that point of chaotic conflict among a few "men," he says it's a matter
of assassination. In the chaos of incommensurate ideas competitors are
killed off. One idea remains and plays like an instrument that brings the

---

5. Wallace Stevens, *The Collected Poems of Wallace Stevens* (New York: Alfred A. Knopf, 1982),
255–56.

mass of meaning and people to ordered composure. The one remaining finds agreement between the mass of people and himself. It's an agreement with night, Stevens says, a temporary agreement, I believe, between a ruling idea and darkness, where neither order nor things are recognizable. The chaos happens in the established order, in the composure and agreement, in the imposition and rule of the single idea consequent to assassination of competing possibilities for establishing ordered formations of sense.

> . . . The assassin sings
> In chaos and his song is a consolation.
> It is the music of the mass of meaning.

In the "blood-world," Stevens says, we cannot find the right sound to bring the mass of meaning to right order. That can happen only by imaginative abstraction where chaos reigns. In this poem Stevens finds in the mass of meaning and people an overall equivalence—meanings and people taken as an aggregate are not governed by singularity; rather, altogether they are characterized by an undifferentiated quality. Nothing rules supreme in its differentiation until a singular one gains control, and that appears to happen only in imaginative order. In such order Stevens finds chaos: killing off the neutrality of mass as well as killing off other wannabe ruling ideas in the fabrication of figures of a dominant order, the invention of a pure singularity, the construction of what we could never find in warm-blooded lives.

Strange, isn't it, to think of indifference in the mass of meaning and of people? And to find the rightness of an order only in an assassin's triumphant and transcendent singularity in which night, not another order, shades as background to the established light! The operation of the law of chaos in Steven's words.

This book begins with a consideration of beauty, indifference, and wisdom. It moves to time and "soul" and finds a turning point with freedom and goodness. F. W. J. Schelling's persistent thought on love and indifference comes next, followed by reflections in the context of indifference on trauma, our bodies, humor, and public memory. A consideration of the strange transition of banality to beauty brings it to a close.

What is at stake for us as we live with a strong sense of indifference in the events of our lives? For some philosophers what is at stake is turning as trained thinkers from their preoccupation with texts to the nontextual and unthinking dimensions of whatever happens. These dimensions exceed the order (and hence control) of meaning. And yet this aspect of living events presents their own happening, their own existence, and defines the limits of intelligence and human significance. I will need to show that such dimensions are in some sense available for recognition and that our attunement to them can make an important difference in the way we live.

As I noted at the beginning of this chapter, our language and habits of thought and speech can effectively blind us to the dimension of indifference in our environments. A second significant factor in addition to turning to the nontextual world is finding ways of speaking and thinking that make this dimension and its importance evident. As you have already seen, forms of expression that are not strictly philosophical might well help us in their exploration of words, conceptions, kinds of indirection, and recognitions of broken connections. These are explorations that make more articulate the attunement and sensibility that this book investigates.

To the extent that people find satisfaction in a sense of unified and systematic wholeness, the third major issue is found in our coming to recognize some of the ways that that satisfaction distances us from the events of our lives. Dimensions of indifference define interruptions of orders as well as limits to our sense of meaning. We will see that living with alertness to the dimension of indifference can help to shape attitudes that are alert to the value of incommensurable differences. At best those attitudes are not inclined to overcome such differences in the interests of orders that in the name of right and goodness add to the misery of people.

We are thus considering a shift in some dominant sensibilities in Western society toward dispositions and expectations that are attuned to neutrality that characterizes our most basic experiences of differentiation. Our meanings and values do not define fully their own occurrences—that is one descriptive claim that guides this book. Another guiding claim is that when people are attuned in their recognitions and actions to this neutrality of living events, a change in sensibility occurs that makes possible changes in some of our most destructive ways of living.

TWO

Helen, Truth, and the Wisdom of Nemesis

A MYTHOLOGICAL BEGINNING

Surely we would be unwise to worship Helen, the compelling, early Greek phantom of calamitous beauty.[1] According to early accounts, she is the daughter of Nemesis, who, when she conceived Zeus's daughter, was a beautiful and unseducible goddess of stern fate. Nemesis, in early myths, figured the circumstances and inevitabilities of offense. She was not at all a flattened image of mere angry vengeance but a much more subtle sensibility of measured consideration, knowing that offense carries consequences as surely as shame follows on desecration and violation. Nemesis did not need or want Zeus, who pursued her relentlessly with a strange sense of erotic destiny. She fell prey as she slept to the onslaught of his passion, she as a wild goose and he as a swan, to her indelible offense and, we can assume, shame—powerful, obscene offense and shame consequent to a divine rape in the form of sheer animal lust and unaware capitulation. Nemesis's sense of rightness in conduct, her sense of measure and propriety, the beauty of her dark, untested, virginal serenity: These were all, we may assume, outraged by divine, deceptive Zeus, and Helen was the issue. A perfectly beautiful issue, calamitous in her perfect beauty in a world unsuited to perfection, dangerous for all to love in her combination of divine necessity, beauty, and force—a strange force, too, out of reach, often irresistible, something like an intangible offense in its inappropriateness for human

---

1. I base these observations on Roberto Calasso's account in *The Marriage of Cadmus and Harmony* (New York: Vintage, 1994), 124–39.

weakness. Helen, in her perfection, inevitably brought disaster to mortals, as is necessary when grasping and holding perfection is at stake.[2]

To make Helen an object of religious practice would provide a stimulus for erecting the scaffolding of her often-destructive destiny in all reaches of people's attitudes and actions. Such fixation itself would constitute an offense to her beauty. Imagine what her followers would be like: They would form beliefs and images that, in their direction toward such perfect yet vaporous beauty, would generate jealousy and obsession before her unpossessable offering—bear these beliefs and images as surely as outrage follows upon physical violation and civil strife follows from uncivil wounding. Zeus's rape of Nemesis, with Aphrodite's full cooperation—the rape of a divine necessity—figures a hologram so complete in its power for mortal offense and paradox that its multiple, limited repetitions, figured by Helen's life, mean no less than continuous stimulus toward violent, possessive desire. This desire is bred by vaporous attraction, one that seems to require sacrifice but not fulfillment and one that threatened civil war even among the Olympians. The very centering and fixation of Helen by acts of worship and by institutions that teach her supremacy would carry forth a destiny of violent offense and would constitute treason before the unfixable mortality of her beauty. To follow her in such a way would instill rapine and violation in the heart of devotion and create spirits of offense to the very beauty from which they took their inspiration. To worship Helen would be to submit to an earthly scaffolding of destructive obsession and sublime superficiality before her beautiful and mortal simulacrum of divine power, limitation, violation, and offense.

"Sublime superficiality" comes across as a contradiction. "Sublime" often suggests exaltation and elevation to something extraordinary and beyond the surface. But in Homer's world—and Homer did not worship Helen—sublimity did not reach beyond surfaces: Appearances opened to other appearances, and he took images of perfection in appearance to be at best godlike. Lives appeared and disappeared, and people might as well make as much of the appearances as they can, because that's all they themselves are and all they have to work with—and disappearances do not provide much by way of workable matter. Sublime events in his world were like vapors of the surface, like sea spray radiant with sunlight, for example, and their moments were all the more beautiful for their expiration.

---

2. Helen's divinity and mortality are ambiguous. For Homer she is quite human. But she was a worshipped goddess in Sparta and Rhodes. I shall play on this ambiguity by applying Calasso's term, simulacrum, which in this context allows for both embodiment and elusive, mythical ideality.

Perhaps in this context there is more in Helen's destiny than the consequences of possessive offense. Perhaps her beauty transposes banal necessity—vaporizes and radiates it—embodies it without redeeming it or defeating it, but embodies and transposes banal necessity with a mesmerizing draw, an allure that leads people to strive and to take far more pleasure in living than the sum total of suffering and death would seem to justify. Perhaps Zeus's divine offense, against all odds, is returned, transfigured with innocent, Homeric pleasure and delight, transformed by poetic imagination, forgiven almost, by an incarnation, not of immortal perfection, but of simple beauty—poetic beauty in Homer's instance—that will die as surely as it is celebrated. Not less than enchanting, not more than an effulgence of flesh and form, perhaps Helen's simulacrum enlivens people without justification. We would be unwise to worship her, but we might be wise to welcome her enchantment as her vaporous beauty emerges in our culture's multiple sensibilities. Short of worship, perhaps we should stop with Helen's simulacrum, with her indifferent luminous, nimbus quality—and she is indeed more nimbuslike than numinous—and find there an unlikely opening to wisdom, if not to Helen's wisdom, to a wisdom that holds her free from all requirements that would circumscribe her.

What are we to say of wisdom in this context? Especially if wisdom is to be figured by mortal time? Helen, after all, appears with many origins—she also comes, for example, from foam hardened into an egg, foam that in its lively fluidity had given birth to Aphrodite. She is linked to mere whiteness, to the white of a swan's egg or a lily and to the isle of Leukos. She is, in her vaporous quality, without substance. Her life is "marked by a moment of precarious, fleeting equilibrium, when, thanks to the deceitful cunning of Zeus, necessity and beauty were superimposed the one over the other."[3] She is cloudlike, enjoying the heavenly quality of sky rather more than the earthly density. And yet this ghostly form, once embodied in an Athenian girl, occasioned a war of mad brutality and deceit as well as a poem of earthly beauty and force. And even in the instance of the Trojan War, there is doubt, framed by Herodotus, whether the "real" Athenian girl, the one Paris found in Sparta and with whom he fled, was behind the Trojan walls and not, instead, in Egypt—there is doubt whether the Helen from Athens and then Sparta was *the* Helen of Troy. Surely the *Iliad* is not formed with a vacuous Helen at its center. Surely this great work is not figured and given motivation by so mortal a nonsubstance as to be blank at its center, as to have a missing core, something there that is less than an excuse, something more like an elision. Is a simulacrum of evasive beauty the origin of Homer's epic?

3. Calasso, *Marriage,* 127.

I do not wish to turn to the whiteness of Homer's page, or to gaze at his pen making marks on it, or to find him poeticizing a body of signs. I think that he is addressing physical events as he writes in elisions and ellipses. And although Homer's writing is formulaic, it is nonetheless, in its conventions, addressed to unique passions, deeds, and human experiences of flesh and blood. It's an address that finds no loss in the absence of universals or a unified cosmos. Homer takes delight in bodies and in the excursions and exaggerations of his specifically Greek language and imagination. As he tells his story he is pleased by sculpted chests and well-formed breasts, by tapered waists and broad shoulders, by skin and texture. And pleased, too, by a mélange of deities who are nothing less than Greeks writ large. My own un-Greek imagination guesses that Homer would have been greatly amused to discover that stars burn out, galaxies eat each other, and people go to economic battle for the privilege of building hamburger stands in foreign lands. Were he to write of such things, he could imbue them with unique life and lightness because, I think, he lived in love with Helen's beauty and understood intimately the meaning of her lightening, quickening power. That meaning did not take the form of stories with moral lessons. It articulated a differently focused way of life, an ethos with delight informed by the indifference of Helen's simulacrum.

I would like to consider wisdom in the phantomlike atmosphere that Helen's allure provides. For wisdom, like Helen's beauty in Nemesis's lineage, might enact no elemental equilibrium, no base of goodness or imperative. It might have to do with surface vacuums, fetters of this or that necessity, specific environments, irreplaceable individuals, social manipulations, and vaporous, conflicted, often brutal, often sublime events and possibilities in our lives. I would like to keep in mind too that Helen figures betrayal as well as beauty, that if she has grace, she has a youthful grace without wrinkles or hair on her chin, that if she inspired great deeds she also inspired mad desire and witless destruction. She transfixes us by the destiny that came with Zeus's offense of her mother, awesome Nemesis, who knew the comportment proper to the limitations of all events. With Nemetic wisdom, however, we might find the manners that must accord with her daughter and accord in such a way that we let her appear without the violations of possessive force. If the Athenians were right, that beauty rules over strength when people are concerned, we will need to find out how we might relinquish—yield to—the most beautiful dimensions of things in order to not trespass them and to allow them their unique and ungraspable powers. It might be that if we do not ask too much of Helen, if we are able to allow and respect her limits, we might find some of her mother's wisdom combined with her beauty.

I fantasize Nemesis, daughter of Night or perhaps faceless Ananke, beautiful Nemesis—before people relegated her only to angry, vicious revenge. I fantasize her at the time when Zeus became obsessed with her, Nemesis, as I said, who figured the delicate proprieties of alert and affirmative sensibility to limits whose overstepping consisted in wounding and inevitable wounding return. She cared for limits, not specifically for entities, but for limits that are as faceless as Ananke and Chronos, and she knew when beings were bound to retaliation—proper retaliation, it would seem. I believe that she, with a sufficiency of integrity and strength that was not incidental to her beauty, enjoyed a self-contained serenity in the retributions that arose with inevitability when boundaries were violated, just as her daughter knew of bonding desire and its inevitabilities with a self-contained serenity that only the beautiful seem to enjoy. True to her mother and to her mother's consort, Chronos, Nemesis is in no sense immoral, and she certainly has much to do with the boundaries necessary for any ethos. She has about her a carefulness, a necessity of attentiveness, a quality that we can view as either dark or shining, a quality of bonding with all the ambiguity of limits: Things are bound to limits, but limits, as they bond, are hardly bound themselves. They simply divide and connect and give definition. With them things are bound to happen—bound to appear, I would say—just as they are, no matter how mutational and conflictual their bounded powers might be. The needless care for limits by Nemesis seems to come with individuations whose mortal stabilities require a certain bondage to boundaries and freedom from destructive invasion. Nemesis knows that when boundaries are violated, the violation itself is bound to bring violence in return so long as the borders remain definitive. Nemesis's wisdom is not found in retribution, but in retribution's inevitability when limits constitutive of things are indiscriminately crossed.

A WORD ON HEIDEGGER
AND TRUTH

With Helen's beauty and Nemesis's wisdom in mind, and with time, limit, and mortality hovering in the background, I turn to Heidegger. I have considered Helen in the unlikely context of wisdom because people often take beauty, especially physical beauty, its pursuit and its enjoyment, to be unfriendly to wisdom or, at best, indifferent and problematic before stern wisdom's demands. I have associated Helen's beauty with lightness and vivification. Her beauty could be associated with her grandmother Ananke's faceless unconcern for things. But given her mother's investment in limits, we have in Helen's beauty both resplendent unconcern for most things *and* a figuration that draws men and women to singular actions by the singularity of her incommensurable physicality. The problem is that people who follow beauty in its many manifestations often, in their dedication, do not care for much else and are capable of the most unseemly disregard for other values. Helen is close by, for example, when a person sacrifices most good things, including active concern for other people's welfare, in a (let us say) successful effort to create a genuine and beautiful work of art. But if some state of mind known as wisdom gets heavy from seriousness and desire for the security of something final that reflects back to it its own image, and if such wisdom becomes enfettered with authority, prominence, and reward, and if such wisdom begins to love itself over all things, then we might have reason to recall Nemesis, and we might look with longing to Helen's passing visage as Nemesis's daughter returns on a light and refreshing breeze. For so-called wisdom cannot trespass Helen's beauty without losing her and losing, too, its truth as wisdom. Before Helen, a wise state of mind meets beauty without wisdom, and with Nemesis as guide a wise state of mind recognizes the danger of violation and the . . . wisdom . . . of reticence, delight, perhaps astonishment before this beauty's wonderful occurrence. Wisdom must be firm and not flee with Helen to some fortress or hidden cave. But with a sense of their own limits, wise people might find their wise lives taking on Helen's nimbic beauty, as though it were given without revenge when her singular physicality is allowed without violation. For Helen cannot be absorbed by wisdom's acts any more than Helen can take wisdom captive. Helen's mother knows that boundaries allow lives their freedom to appear and that violation of this freedom is never wise.

To think of Heidegger listening to Helen's laughter carried on a breeze, especially as he is thinking, stretches my imagination. But I find, nonetheless, appropriateness in returning to some pre-Socratic Greek experiences when Heidegger's thought is a significant part of the conversation. Helen is not altogether inappropriate in such a conversation since Heidegger was suspicious of the often-enfettering Western value of wisdom and its frequent claims to power. His accounts of truth and being bring with them a sense of lightness and vital origination that I find much closer to Helen than to, say, many traditional appropriations of Plato and Aristotle. I emphasize that, in contrast to Heidegger's approach to the pre-Socratics, I have focused on the finite simulacrum of Helen's image. I have not given priority to the question of being, and I have taken a more traditional view of Greek ideas of necessity and destiny than Heidegger takes and one that is not sympathetic to his thought of *Geschick*. But I think that we might well consider wisdom in the context of Heidegger's thought of aletheic events, and I think that what I have called Nemesis's wisdom in Helen's regard is very much to the point when we consider the virtues and limits that compose wisdom's enactment by reference to Heidegger's account of truth.

Aletheia: the concealing-unconcealing enactment of things. Concealing: everything that happens, in its disclosive happening, enjoys its own incommensurability, occurs as its own irreducible self-disclosure, and eventuates in withdrawal from all encompassing figurations. Being, the enactment of all things, loves to hide, if Heidegger's Heraclitus is right, and this hiding, this concealment, carries through as being's ungraspableness—it cannot be identified as anything determinate, and the hiddenness of being is also carried through as an insubstantial, fleeting dimension in the lives of all things. Concealment—the *lethe* of *aletheia*—means also a clearing away and unburdening quality as things occur, leaving a wake of unholdable eventuations.

Unconcealing: things are there, appearing, available for experience, perception, engagement, *there* without a determinate, unified sufficiency of origin, quite remarkably there before reasons and interpretations apply. There at once determinately and indeterminately in their events. Things, Heidegger says, show themselves. They in their unconcealment compose the world. Unconcealing is like "letting lie before," like allowance for things' rising up and being there, and for Heidegger that is like a gift of determinate life. Heidegger seemed to be surprised that the world is here at all, and part of that surprise—sometimes delighted surprise—finds expression in the emphasis that he gives to unconcealment.

Aletheia: events without a sub-stance. Events are light in their densities in the sense that in their being they come to pass, in the sense that in their presence no perfection of defining presence occurs to compromise the limits of their mortal passage; light in the sense that the eventuation of things grants no presence other than the presencing of events.

I would like to highlight in these thoughts of Heidegger the Helen-like aspect of ephemeral beauty and the Nemesis-like aspect of limit, the violation of which brings calamity. Perhaps, in this complex, we will find something of wisdom that discerns beauty in the limited eventuation of things and discerns such beauty with judgments that arise from a discrete apprehension of inviolate boundaries. Perhaps we will also find a wisdom that is predisposed toward physical beauty—beauty in the eventuation, the unconcealing of things—and predisposed as well to know that such beauty is outside of wisdom's control. People are wise in knowing that beauty is different from wisdom.

Helen-like. I have followed Calasso's presentation of Helen as a simulacrum, as a phantom-embodiment of fateful, physical beauty with the quality of a hologram, fateful beauty that withdraws from any finally definitive form beyond physical occurrences. His judgment—and I believe this to be a wise judgment—is that Helen's physical beauty, as physical and belonging to surfaces, has in it an elusive intangibility that tangibly draws people with passion. Her presence is enchanting in part because of its perfection in its ever-withdrawing, ever-forthcoming phantom-dimension. Helen's beauty is not possessable, even by her. It is always cropping up—emerging—in Greek experience, and emerging, I believe, in myths and literature because people found it again and again in their lives. Calasso's work is on myths, and a person might well say that the simulacrum he finds has its place of occurrence in a mythical realm that provides enough distance from day-to-day living to allow a concourse for gods and people. But were myths separated from ordinary lives and were mythical repetitions only in stories, their meanings would be at best irrelevantly idealistic. Myths arise from the surfaces of lives, gloss them and repeat them and return to them; and Helen's simulacra bespeak the surfaces where they belong. They articulate a lively limit that people wisely respect when they do not turn Helen into one circumscribable reality—the one most beautiful woman—or into an object of worshipful adoration.

Heidegger says that in largely hidden crevasses of the Western tradition we can find a most remarkable attunement with the insubstantial arising-passing of events. We are attuned with things in their occurrences as they come to appear. They happen with an alluring intangibility that bears no less than their own appearing. The necessity of this intangibility is in its happening and not elsewhere. That things happen at all is, I believe, beautiful for Heidegger, and he finds this beauty attended to and addressed in Greek sensibility. It is the beauty of the very happening of beings, of the appearing eventuation of beings. People's attunement with disclosive eventuation inheres in the eventuation of their own lives. It composes a living alertness with eventuating things and with what we can neither grasp nor appropriately objectify.

Allure might be too strong for our aletheic attunement on Heidegger's terms. Perhaps such attunement is too faint, too burdened by distractions, too problematic at a time when Helen seems far gone in a largely dead antiquity. On the other hand, not a small part of Helen's allure is in its secrecy as far as those under its power are concerned. It does have a concealed quality, even when it appears most forcefully, and her allure seems to carry forth as intangibly as a destiny—a faceless destiny—as it exercises its largely unreflective draw.

The aletheic force of things: their concealing-revealing events, their rising up to be, the disclosive force in each thing's being *there,* and, as far as *its* happening is concerned, irreplaceably so: It could be that with all our distractions and preoccupations we are drawn nonetheless by the sheer happening of things, drawn by originary, aletheic happenings. Does such a draw constitute Helen's allure? If we quiet ourselves, genuinely pause before events, their quality of happening will occasion in us, perhaps, a sense of unpossessable beauty. At least I think that Heidegger at times writes out of that kind of experience as he finds it embodied in Greek language. I would not want to universalize this experience, any more than I would want to universalize Helen's allure. But when people experience events in the beauty of their happening, I would say that Helen's simulacrum is at work. And I am saying also that in it plays a destiny of alluring beauty, multiply figured, that has moved people in multiple ways, sometimes disastrously, sometimes not, a beauty that is always elusive and found in ellipses, a beauty that appears lost in its many definitions.

THE WISDOM OF NEMESIS

Nemesis-like. To say that Zeus messed with fate when he raped Nemesis puts the point mildly. Helen was the issue of this divine errancy. There is an aspect of her grandmother's facelessness and her divine father's errancy in her fate. She seems heedless of the consequences that her beauty brings for people, heedless of the human disasters that follow in her wake. The violence and violation of her conception are carried by this heedlessness, this indifference. Her surface beauty carries an imperative no more than *aletheia* does, as Heidegger finds it. But her beauty does carry lightness and brightness in a context of unadorned necessity and impenetrable darkness. I suppose we could say that Helen and *aletheia* have in common no care for the consequences of appearing and its intrinsic allure. Yet each is violable, able to be violated. Helen's body is certainly subject to violation—Theseus sodomized her when she was twelve, for example—and one also has the sense that care for Helen, however she is found, in her limitations, requires close attention and allowance for her mercurial, youthful unpossessability. A limit is violated whenever eventuations are taken as though they were mere objects of cognition or use, just as we miss Helen when we grab her, as it were, or lock her in a fortress with our mothers as guardians, as hapless Theseus did—I imagine that, if confronted by the elusive beauty of *aletheia*, he might squint, spit, and say, what beauty?

People violate the limits of revealing-concealing as they plunge ahead with indiscriminate actions of control and with no sense for what in lives is delicate, not to be used, not within people's grasp and always lost when taken. The fate of such vast insensitivity and misattunement is not unlike that when a child is sodomized: Something irretrievable is lost, something too ugly for words fixes a mark in the world, something to be held in secret is killed by tortured display, and, in this case, a man's gross indelicacy, though triumphant, releases neither joy nor pleasing affection. Heidegger calls such injustice, written large in Western culture, technology. And by his light I would say that Nemesis's presence is felt as the lightness and brightness of things' eventuations fade into the diminished life of domination in unwisely controlled environments.

Neither Helen nor *aletheia* compose moral presence, but both offer what nothing else gives: a quality of vivification, useless astonishment, a dimension of occurrence without command, surfaces of beauty outside the reach of subjects, intentions, or purposes. And Nemesis's fateful wisdom holds for those qualities and dimensions: If people violate them there is a cost of returned violence and violation as surely as when we offend a tribal leader by abusing her child or when we forget the aletheic dimension of all occurring things by treating them purely instrumentally. I think that calamities followed Helen as people attempted in various ways to keep her present. For my part, I think that Helen is to be loved in all her beauty— never ignored—but left unfettered and unkept. I think too that Heidegger describes a dimension of events to which we may attend best without judgment or demand. Ethical and political intelligence will not come from either Helen or *aletheia,* although ethical and political judgments in the diminishment of something like Helen's simulacrum and *aletheia*'s release will tend fatefully to enfetter people, to weigh them down, unwisely, in the loss of a kind of freedom that only disciplined and appreciative attunement to elusive beauty and *aletheia* allows. Enforcements and habits, authorities and requirements, are not necessarily antithetical to such freedom. They become unwise, rather, in their enshrinements, in elevations of them beyond their ethnic surfaces and their own mortal events. Ethical and political wisdom includes disciplined attentiveness to what cannot be done, to what was never done, and to what, like a simulacrum, seems always to enact itself without virtue and without a fixable origin or identity. Like Helen. Like *aletheia* as Heidegger accounts it.

The struggle between moral judgment and nonjudgmental perception is an old one for us Westerners. I think that we would be wise to see that when either kind of awareness violates the borders of the other, people inevitably suffer major losses in the quality of their lives, that something like Nemesis stares vacantly in the depletion, neither sad nor happy, knowing, as it were, that indiscriminate trespass brings indiscriminate death, even— perhaps especially—if the trespasser is an ethical system or a political institution. The wisdom of Nemesis in this context comes with an alert sensibility that is predisposed to know that both Helen's beauty and *aletheia* are outside of the circumscription of ethical and political intention. We might also wisely know that efforts to incorporate them into our ethical and political formations will come under Nemesis's awful jurisdiction. A faceless in-dignation will arise in which life diminishes, goodness spoils, and cultures become agencies of banal ugliness.

Let's look at this struggle between moral judgment and indifferent per-ception in the context of Pythagorean teaching and practice. How might people think of the soul as a site of beauty, truth, and differentiation?

THREE

Pythagoras, Indifference, and the Beautiful Soul

She need not judge. There did not have to be a moral.
She need show only separate minds, as alive as her own,
struggling with the idea that other minds were equally alive.
It wasn't only wickedness and scheming that made people
unhappy, it was confusion and misunderstanding; above all,
it was the failure to grasp the simple truth that other people
are as real as you. And only in a story could you enter these
different minds and show how they had an equal value.
That was the only moral a story need have.

—Ian McEwan, *Atonement*

To understand the sense of memory in Orphic and Pythagorean practice and thought we need to consider experiences of ignorance. I don't have in mind only a lack of information. I'm thinking of a sense of ignorance in a context of knowing that being alive is mostly a matter of misery and unhappiness, frequent sickness, infection, and unrelieved pain; simple not-knowing with depression and boredom, fear; mindless repetition, work that breaks down bodies. And staring ignorantly before occasional moments of transcendence in which people feel no pain or sorrow or fear. Ignorance in hearing rare people who hold vast stores of ordered words in their minds, who give accounts of undying things and who know the secrets of serenity, peace, and life without change. We should hold in mind, too, not knowing why water comes from the sky, the earth sometimes shakes, wind blows, and beautiful things disappear. To understand the sense of memory in Orphic and Pythagorean practice and thought, we need to think of lives lived without the order of writing, of stories that give at once order and order's breakdown, of stories of wild and tempestuous things that no story can hold. And, of strange things: blood, intoxication, dead things with things springing from them alive. When we think of ignorance we should think of dumbness—muteness—in a world that holds but does not seem to hear or care for people's stories about it. Is there Someone there who hears or cares? Some order of preservation? Is there something we can do to erase the chaos or to give us an edge, a knowledge of the way that avoids disaster? What holds still long enough for us to know it? What lasts long enough to conquer death? How do we reach that still point that we can sometimes almost feel, a point that seems to hold steady with a life that is indifferent—unthreatened, unmoved—by the sum of human catastrophe? How might we hold things and ourselves still? Still enough to know fully, to see completely, to overcome change? Still enough not to deteriorate? Not to die?

The sense of memory that I would like to consider in the context of seventh- and sixth-century B.C.E. Greek culture constitutes the opposite of ignorance. It—memory—came as a vaguely maternal promise of salvation and then, in Plato, transformed into a form of nonritualized knowledge. Throughout this process, the indifference of the cycle of mortality and careless eternity remains constant, and ignorance is defined by the circumscription of generation and decay, and hence the need for care.

A simple discipline that Pythagoras recommended—that of recalling at the end of each day what a person has done and left undone—is neither as simple nor as strictly psychological as it might seem to us.[1] He is requiring a practice of memory whose purpose is only secondarily to allow people to come to know themselves. It is primarily a practice by which a nonmortal agency might come to force, an agency without ignorance, the very presence of Mnemosyne. "The very presence of Mnemosyne" is an awkward

---

1. What Pythagoras in fact said or wrote is beyond reasonable determination. There are no extant documents that are clearly written by him. Many reports about him and what he said are available, however, and when I speak of "Pythagoras" I am referring to such reports. There are many discussions of these sources. Those that I have consulted include the following: Charles H. Kahn, *Pythagoras and the Pythagoreans: A Brief History* (Indianapolis: Hackett, 2001); Jean-Pierre Vernant, *Myth and Thought among the Greeks* (London: Routledge, 1983) and *Mortals and Immortals* (Princeton, N.J.: Princeton University Press, 1991); Jane Ellen Harrison, *Prolegomena to the Study of Greek Religion* (Princeton, N.J.: Princeton University Press, 1992); Kathleen Freeman, *Companion to the Pre-Socratic Philosophers* (Oxford: Basil Blackwell, 1953); Eduard Zeller, *Outlines of the History of Greek Philosophy* (New York: Meridian, 1955); Alexander P. D. Mourelatos, ed., *The Pre-Socratics* (New York: Doubleday, 1974); David B. Claus, *Toward the Soul: An Inquiry into the Meaning of* Psyche *before Plato* (New Haven, Conn.: Yale University Press, 1981); Gregory Vlastos, "Theology and Philosophy in Early Greek Thought," *Philosophical Quarterly* 2, no. 7 (1952); and Marcel Detienne, *The Masters of Truth in Archaic Greece* (New York: Zone, 1996). Omar Rivera, at my request, made many helpful suggestions concerning sources, and wrote an unpublished paper, "Pythagoreanism and Orphism," from which I have drawn ideas for content and approach to this topic.

phrase because she rules the unchanging past. She is not, however, a holder of past events. In addition to the goddess of memory, she is the unchanging power of affiliation with the unchanging. Pythagoras wanted his adherents to awaken an available if obscure immortal power, to awaken themselves to it, to open into a chamber where their many past lives are evident in their departures from their own deathless principle, and to learn—to remember—the way to deathless life.

The attachment of a sense of ignorance to a sense of mortality has a vast period of development. It reaches, I speculate, far beyond the life of writing, reaching into the early formation of many emotions that seem definitive of people. In my approach to Pythagorean thought, I will highlight only three aspects of this strange and wonderful lineage of knowledge concerning mortals and immortals, a lineage that in its recitation dispels ignorance and brings not only knowledge of the Divines but divine knowledge as well. The three aspects are memorized and recited genealogies, access to timeless presence by means of memory, and the ritual functions of Orphic cults.

First is the significance of trained memory. Jean-Pierre Vernant emphasizes in his observations on trained memory the social significance of ordering and enumerating past things. Genealogies of rulers, horses, weapons, successes, and gods tell a people where they came from and who they are.[2] And he emphasizes as well the sense-giving attachment of order among past things, origins, gods, and immutability. By an act of memory these verbally communicated lists provided ordered clarity where there was for most people the simple oblivion of no memory, no sense of identity. They gave specificity by determination of the past. Ordered words! A certain harmony of words! Genealogical knowledge generates a sense of continuity and a knowledge of what doesn't change. Further, what might sound aporetic to our ears—that discovery of *past* things and beginnings uncovers timelessness—describes exactly what a talented seer or poet came to enact with Mnemosyne's divine guidance: The poet or seer ascertains deathless beginnings, immortal truths, and unchanging, sacred messages by means of the psyche's memory, a memory, I suppose, that was aided considerably by a prodigious and ordered capacity to recite, and to recite without discernible error in spite of the changing years. In such poetic and memorial sight people collectively and as individuals come to know who they are now and what sense their lives and the cosmos generally have. That sense came with a sense of eternity, of unchangeableness, and came as well with its difference from a world in which change and thus suffering and death are in-

2. Vernant, *Mortals and Immortals*, chapter 3.

evitable. Eternity, with its difference from contingency, changes for no one. Neither do the inevitabilities of change, suffering, and death in a world of contingency. Eternity is sacred indifference before all human cares, and mutable temporality is profane indifference in the inevitability of those cares. We could add that the difference between them might be called mere indifference.

In addition to these recited, society-forming senses of lineage, eternity, and time, Vernant emphasizes that the past, discovered by the trained psyche in early Greek culture, is past only for those of us caught in the ignorance of temporal existence. The seer-poet's psyche discovers an eternal present. "We step outside of our own human universe and discover behind it other regions of being, other cosmic levels normally inaccessible to us."[3] Memory is the power to step outside of our normal world. It composes, in essence, a nontemporal function by a nontemporal agency that can discover its kinship with otherwise hidden deathlessness. This sense of memory is one of seeing now for always. And it was with this sense that Pythagoras trained his devotees to begin their journey of soul by remembering themselves in the passing day's events. It was a small beginning toward the gift of *anamnesis* and the joining of beginning and end in Mnemosyne's singular goodness.

A third aspect that I am noting in the lineage of mortals and immortals is found in the functions of cults. There is broad agreement among classical specialists that there was an important Orphic influence on the thought of Pythagoras and hence on that of Plato. And Orphic religion was cultic. By "cultic" I mean ritualized religious practice as distinct from philosophical conception. Jane Harrison states the point nicely: "The Orphics faced the most barbarous elements of their own faith [past practices of human sacrifice] and turned them not only qua [a largely mythologized] theology into a vague monotheism, but qua ritual into a high sacrament of spiritual purification."[4] The goal of Orphic practice that is especially relevant for this discussion is its translation by processes of purification of people's souls from ignorance to alert communion with spiritual entities and finally its translation of thoroughly cleansed souls into divinities. These translation processes are primarily by means of ritual practices, and that means Orphic asceticism in the form of dietary regimens and curtailment of corrupting practices, especially sexual ones—those ascetic practices had their meaning in the purification of souls and not in, say, a general improvement of the world for the world's sake. The point was to leave the world and its deathli-

3. Vernant, *Mortals and Immortals*, 80.
4. Harrison, *Prolegomena*, 481.

ness by the force of a transformed soul, and at best temporal life is a process of learning how to live by the nontemporal beat of a person's immortal part. In Orphic culture, to be bad is to be impure, and the punishment for impurity is in the inevitable, indifferent cycle of returning to impure, ignorant, and suffering existence.

The Orphic cult constituted not only ritualized practices of psychic translation. It also constituted a transformation of many ancient Dionysian cultic practices. This is a transformation that we would probably unanimously agree is progressive, or if you are shy about using the word progressive, a salutary refinement. One of the practices that the Orphics refined was that of human sacrifice, especially sacrifice of beautiful children. Orphic rituals also brought together Dionysian resurrection, which previously had to do with eating the living, that is, bleeding, flesh of a human or animal—the Orphics brought that ritual to a slightly more modern state of celebrating a memorial meal, first probably with raw meat or a ritually killed animal, and thereby joined memory, resurrection, and eternity into an anamna-ascetic union whereby the soul, in re-membering cleansed and past cultic practices, participates purely in a translation to new, deathless life.

I emphasize this transforming process because it itself constitutes a major influence in its time. This process marks a way in which cultic, mythological values and entities continue with force in changed, ritual practices. In this case meanings of bloody sacrifices continue in memorial practices that reconstitute the rituals but that hold the values intended by the earlier performances. And, as we shall see, the Orphic rites constitute a *movement* that allows for a *theoretical* transformation of those very rituals. So we may say that the Orphic rituals themselves hold a *movement* of transformation from the practices of human blood sacrifices, and in that dynamic dimension, they communicate the uncommon value of holding past values and meanings in place by means of present memorial acts. The Orphic rites were memorial as they enacted the memory of communion with gods by means of human flesh or the living flesh of bulls. And they as well as Pythagorean practices were transformative as they required a *continuing* purification of devotees' *souls*. Their transforming contribution came with their emphasis on soul and psychic purification with a consequent emphasis on the individual. But they continued to ferment the Dionysian and ancient brew consisting in the values assigned to salvation, purification, and special knowledge. It was a libation designed to eliminate ignorance that in Orphic care turned Dionysian intoxication and flowing blood into memorial enactments whose purpose was delivery of the psyche's immortal inheritance.

Pythagoras, on the other hand, was not so much a priest as he was a teacher and theoretician. In his teachings a transformation of the ancient myths took place in which soul practices combined with theoretical observations to form cults more like schools of secret knowledge than temples of ritual sacrifice.

The thematic aspects to follow are (1) a paramount value given to purity of soul; (2) a teaching of soul-memory; (3) the intimacy of memory, knowledge, and immortality; and (4) the definitive ignorance constitutive of mutable time. Wherever we find these four aspects in classical Greece and the lineages that follow it, we may be reasonably certain that we are in the wake of Orphic and Pythagorean emphases. The originality of Pythagoras and Plato is found in part in the ways they redressed these aspects and carried them into the center of their philosophical conceptions.

Pythagoras was a mathematician, philosopher, and religious sage. He apparently considered his mathematical knowledge to be a teaching most properly secreted among the select of his followers. Such knowledge held the secrets of the cosmos and was conveyed in almost a cultic manner, but it also was rigorously and intellectually formulated as distinct to poetic and mythological. And people, to fully understand such knowledge, required souls purified by ascetic practices. Like Orphic saints, Pythagoras enjoyed quasi-divine status. Many miracles were attributed to him, and his many, remembered past lives were much noted among the initiated. Most significantly, his knowledge addressed quests for salvation, and "salvation" means for a soul an end of its time, a return to its origin, and a release from its exile in bodies. Perhaps in available literature and with proper qualification, Socrates as presented in the *Phaedo* best exemplifies a probable fulfillment of Pythagorean translation into a divine state.

Harrison describes the cardinal teachings of Orphic religion as presenting the way for souls to attain divine life.[5] This is also a primary conviction in Pythagorean thought: People can reach by means of purification a divine life, one appropriate for souls, and one that is characterized by knowledge of the unchanging nature of all definitive things cosmological and soul-connected. "Soul-connected" is ambiguous insofar as the term does not allow us to decide whether souls are separate from people's identities or are constitutive of them. That's a complicated issue that I shall not address other than to note that (1) in comparison with Olympian religion we have in Orphic and Pythagorean thought a distinct turn to individuals and to their availability for immortality and communion with immortal things; (2) immortality and individual ways of living are intimately tied together for both Orphics and Pythagoreans; (3) there is now apparent a forceful and individ-

5. Harrison, *Prolegomena*, 477.

ualized connection between purity and proper ethos; and (4) the soul has primary value for thought and ethos—*the* thing is undying life; life free of the ignorance enforced by temporal limits; life as a seamless, eternal circle, shining like a star, in which beginning and end are always already one and without need of conjunction. Orphic and Pythagorean practices have as their overwhelming goal the soul's salvation from physical time, and their emerging insight is that communities and states need to be formed according to the requirements of souls' divine lives.

The early seer-poets, who at one time gave order to past things and made manifest a people's identity, and the later seer-poets, who revealed timeless things in the merciful justice of Mnemosyne's wisdom, have now transformed. We have priests, teachers, and thinkers who see eternal order through their own immortal agency and provide the outlines for soul-order that should guide the directions of human societies. The special one who sees beyond time, who can think and formulate in regard to this beyond, who is untainted by corruption (or almost so), and who practices the merciful justice of sharing privileged knowledge has taken the shape of hope for suffering people. The Orphics and Pythagoreans ushered in an era for souls in which people could feel the availability of immortality *for them,* the availability of life without pain or ignorance. That special knowledge that gave individuals an opening to new, personal status would contribute not only to the great struggles for personal freedom and public justice but also to those horrors bred of special knowledge that is formulated in a sense of moral uprightness, immortality's availability, and the priority of souls untainted by physicality.

I turn now directly to a consideration of Pythagorean thought with an emphasis on the indifference of the site of knowledge and of that which is to be known, an indifference that constitutes the soul in its perfection and also characterizes that upon which soul-enhancing knowledge fixes its attention. I turn also to the remarkable difference that such indifference makes. When I say "indifference," I mean an absence of any semblance of divine care and the correlated elevation of an image of the soul as essentially careless. The soul's proper concern in the world is oriented by the soul's uncaring transcendence of the world. If I am right in finding a definitive connection among suffering, senses of ignorance, and the salvific knowledge of the Orphics and Pythagoreans, the issue of indifference in soul, body, and eternity becomes pronounced. I will state the issues in four formulations:

1. Indifference characterizes all impersonal inevitabilities. Classical images of fate, for example, and, more relevant for Orphic and Pythagorean symbolization, of Chronos present a sense of complete im-

personality. The same can be said for mortal time. Life in its necessities, both immortal and mortal, appears to be definitively uncaring, and, in the broad sensibility that we are considering, all kinds of care would seem to constitute something added to life qua life.

2. The path to salvation for Orphics and Pythagoreans is indifferent in the sense that whoever you are, queen or bricklayer, you must achieve a certain priority of soul and quality of soul-knowledge or you will be ignorant and your soul could well inhabit in the next life the flesh of a miserable cur or slave without good prospects for salvation anytime soon.

3. On the other hand, a significant difference is made if you do give yourself over to purification and the discipline of remembrance. If you care enough to do that, your soul might achieve its perfection, or if not perfection you might come to love divine things and experience considerable improvement in soul-knowledge and the benefits that it brings. The point is that the soul's own rightful and perfect state is without care in the sense that, like a golden nugget, it is simply hidden without reach or desire in a corruption of flesh and ignorant figurations of life. Desire for it and care that gives it to shine are found in the suffering individual and not in soul's own-most being.

4. When we confront Pythagoras, we confront as well a considerable tradition in which contemplation of uncaring and deathless things appears to work to the considerable benefit of the contemplators and often those in the contemplators' environment. This is a lineage in which a manner of abasement or sacrifice or attendance to beings that do not care seems to produce important knowledge and to be salutary for people. There are, of course, other traditions built around gods who pay considerable attention to people and make a considerable fuss over what they do morally and how they do it, but those lineages are less directly apparent in Orphic and Pythagorean thought.

By these observations I am noting a connection between noncaring being, knowledge of it, and differences in lives that such knowledge can make. Something fine, or genuine beauty and perfection, can eventuate when people learn to attend carefully to immortal, careless life. The transformation and harmonization of life—a transformation of ignorance to true knowledge that makes a huge difference and fulfills the deepest human desire for uninterrupted, tranquil being—such transformation is effected as people give up everything else for the priority of the soul that, at its best, knows without care or imprint of change.

Numbers are so clear. Their harmonious and proportioned connections are so pure. Even their fractional divisions are without irritation and discord. In the huge storms that sweep the Mediterranean coasts there is the still and windless dimension where numbers are the necessary and sufficient realities to determine in complete tranquility each part and the whole of the disturbance. As two walls of men in battle savagely slash and tear each other, the rise of each sword and each micromovement of the rise are defined by the tranquil face of numerical relations. Numbers and their connections, with no passion, no odor, no imperfection of sight, no blemish or putrefaction—numbers present a region so perfect, so transcendent that they need no attribution of either movement or nonmovement.

Think of Pythagoras or Philolaus or Theophrastus, or draw the image of some otherwise nameless and unfigured follower. Think of one of them measuring by thought the relations of lines, planes, points, angles, and surfaces, measuring by invariant principles—seeing mentally (are we already in the soul's space?) with mathematical calculation the very measure of volume and dimension, the fixed range of whole space, the harmony of sound and cosmic proportionality. Think of the silence of this revelatory space, the need for quietness of mind for a strange manner of listening, for concentration without distraction. An entire life suggests itself in the stillness of this sight—not sight, exactly, but like the unfolding of cosmic dimension, step by rigorous step, one connection after another, sometimes slowly, at other times instantly, but *archai* upon *archai* emerge, smooth, so tranquil, so much like something enacting itself with no remainder. *It* takes over. He stands in awe, something wordless emerges, harmonious, proportionately splendid, shining, perfect, matchless, whole, no words. The dog barks. The insistent pain in his lower stomach. He feels himself blinking. Something past. He saw the angles perfected with their lines in a cosmic whole of proportion. He had seen it before. He writes slowly: Today I saw it again. It never changes. The cosmos fitted together. Harmony. Unity. Order. Fit. Limit without limit. The poor creature next door barked just as I saw the whole. It knew. Could his be the ancient Theon's soul?

I am emphasizing two cardinal Pythagorean principles: the soul's immortal destiny and "the role of mathematics as the key for unlocking the secrets of the cosmos, two of the great themes also found in Plato's work."[6] I have placed these emphases in the context of what I might vaguely call "onto-

---

6. Kahn, *Pythagoras and the Pythagoreans*, 50.

logical indifference" and the relevance it has in the Pythagorean direction for differentiating people's lives. I will close with a reflection on a fragment that comes from the work of the Pythagorean Archytas, the great mathematician and statesman who probably saved Plato's life by persuading Dionysus of Syracuse to allow Plato to return to Athens. Archytas also might well have been a major influence on Plato's conception of the importance of mathematics for education in the *Republic* and on many of his conceptions in the *Timaeus*.

"When calculation (or reasoning, *logismos*) is discovered," he said, "it puts an end to civil strife and reinforces concord. Where this is present, greed disappears and is replaced by equality (or fairness, *isotes*). It is by calculation that we are able to come to terms in dealings with one another. By this means do the poor receive from the affluent and the rich give to the needy, both parties believing that by this they will have what is fair (*isom*)."[7]

To the extent that we hear "calculation" to mean "to determine by mathematical processes," this translation of *logismos* is not too misleading. If we understand "calculation" to mean an exercise of practical judgment, however, I believe that we will have difficulty seeing what Archytas's words mean. He might have been a thoroughly secular thinker, as Freeman says and Kahn implies. But I doubt it. I suspect that there is no thoroughly secular or "modern" rational thought in Pythagoreanism of that time, at least not in any sense common now. I suspect that *logismos* means at once both a rational, mathematical process and one in which numbered cosmic harmony announces itself in a soul-nurturing event, an event where timeless, careless, and deathless being, round as Chronos's snake-circle, happens manifestly and gives sensitive and suffering people to turn toward it and seek accord with it as it answers something definitive and hidden in their souls.

Archytas, I speculate—for what else is there to do with fragments?—knew this well: When people form themselves by the purifying discipline of mathematics, and when they come to know the harmony of the whole cosmos, their souls take on a previously unknown shine—a "glory" in the early sense of "great beauty"—and in the light of this uncorrupted resplendence their bodies can adopt a measured calmness that arises only by attention to the soul, a calmness unattracted by greed or the physical satisfactions of power, one without anxiety before death, and one that can practice compassion for those who are struggling to go beyond their ignorance. This would be a compassion that knows its own physical ignorance and knows too the harmonious order that awaits the loss of corruptible time. Such people await the intensity of their souls, attend to a sense of life quite other

---

7. Kahn, *Pythagoras and the Pythagoreans*, 47. His translation.

to the careful sensibility of their everyday lives, and in this attention to *harmonia* they attempt always to serve the interests of beautiful order. They do not want to profit from anything impure, and "impure" means dissonant with the numbered proportionality of the whole that is manifest to the *logismoi,* the people who know the measure of cosmic beauty.

It is also true, consistent with Archytas's sentences, that the world in its essential and numbered proportionality is at least partially receptive to that justice in which each part plays its proper role. Pythagorean knowledge encourages the use of mathematically trained intelligence to determine and distribute the values that form the tissue of a society. But at the level of real controversy—the relations of will, desire, and intelligence, and in this context, the relation of soul and flesh—it is soul-training that counts for the genuine transformation of social relations, and the soul finds through its own, undistracted enactment the one thing with which it is essentially kin: the pure, indifferent beauty of what never changes in limit or order. The deathlessness of perfect and numerical proportion—surely one of the most tempting visions in the West—such beauty turns the ensouled individual to know that nothing else has legitimate claim upon life. The soul composes its own imperative. A person's task is to form the simulacra of the soul's beauty in all situations, and when there is success the environment will be as beautiful as deathly things can be: The society will be ensouled. As well as numbered.

On the one hand, the well-nurtured soul in this context seems to be at one with the indifference of cosmic order. On the other, such a soul is a major factor of differentiation in the temporal world. This combination of indifference and differential power in the essential site of perceptive life set a direction in Western culture that informs modern senses of time and obligation. I will turn now to focus more explicitly on a sensed dimension of indifference that figures philosophical problems about subjectivity and nontheoretical issues for our sense of human vitality and its meaning.

FOUR

The Indifference of Finitude: Arendt and Heidegger

The thought of Hannah Arendt and Martin Heidegger will provide the foci for this chapter. I shall address some of their texts in the context of a problematic that, in part, I bring to them and that, in part, arises in their thought. Let me begin by saying a few words about this problematic.

In addressing what we call finitude, I speak of more than a definitively limited occurrence. I address apparent inevitability—inevitability of individuation and difference, loss and illusion, beginning and ending, concern and need, ambiguity and ambivalence. I speak also of mourning, dispersion, incompletions, pleasures, moments, apertures of meaninglessness, eradication of fulfillments, affections, the draw of the unknown and unknowable. And, important for this discussion, I address the apparent inevitability of thinking. When I speak of what we call finitude, I do not address a category, idea, trope, or definition. I do not address an essence, subject, or an object. I address the apparent and living occurrences of things and people and their places of life.

The strange but ordinary inevitability of finitude composes our lives and the lives of whatever appears. I shall discuss finitude primarily in the context of occurrences of thinking. That is a limited region to be sure, but one nonetheless where finitude's qualities are apparent. As we think with our attention primarily on the finitude of our thinking, we might well begin to think that even the flexible word *finitude* says too much and too little. We might find that the liveliness of thinking in the very aspects I named when I began the chapter—in incompletions, pleasures, and apertures of meaninglessness, for example—the very liveliness of thinking might unsettle us, give us pause, and stir us to fall silent in unexpected ways. This liveliness, when we pay attention to it, might seem to ask for changes in our language and the manner in which we think.

The word *finitude,* in describing not only our thought but also all aspects of our lives, means not just the likelihood of our having to care for everything we value. It also means neutrality that lacks active qualities, radical neutrality with all values, identities, and differences—simple nondifferentiation with differences. The word also suggests the occurrence of individuated differences. How might we think of indifference with inevitable differentiations and nonreducible differences? This connection of indifferent neutrality and the concerns that come with individuation appears with the word *finitude* when we give our attention to the occurrence of what we call finitude. How might we, as we concern ourselves reflectively with finitude, also think (of) its unconcerned indifference? An expectation that motivates this chapter is that finitude will not be a represented object or a presenting subject. It requires a way of thinking that is not circumscribed by representation. I expect also that giving attention to the indifference of finitude will help our effort to address the thought (of) finitude and to find a language appropriate to the address. Further, what difference might an attentive regard for finitude and for the word *finitude* have in the ways we live? These questions both address and express an ethos of finitude.

In the process of following these questions I will need to hold firmly to the difference between finitude, which I doubt occurs with any meaning, and the meaning of the word *finitude,* which is rich and diversified. By operative alertness with this difference I hope to speak and think indirectly of finitude, which, I expect, we may not appropriately say operates or performs a function.

ARENDT: WHAT MAKES US THINK?

Arendt's rendering of Heidegger's question *Was heißt denken?* as What makes us think? places emphasis on a kind of action and production.[1] "Makes," with its sense of production and causation, is not like "call," as in What calls for thinking? Or in What is called thinking? Nor is it quite like "mean," as in What does thinking mean? Thinking generates meanings, according to Arendt. What makes us think is found by her in a basic absence of meaning in our ordinary common sense and our intelligent experiences. In her terminology we think in part because the truth of what we know and the certainties that we believe lack meaning. It's one thing to know what is there and how to use it. It is quite another to have an articulate sense for

---

1. Hannah Arendt, *The Life of the Mind* (New York: Harcourt Brace Jovanovich, 1971). Abbreviated as *LM.* Parenthetical page numbers in this section refer to *LM.* "What Makes Us Think" is the title of the third chapter. I will direct my remarks primarily to this book where Arendt gives her most sustained account of thinking.

what it means. Adolf Eichmann, for example, had reasonably good common sense within the context in which he functioned, and he had skilled knowledge of the intricate bureaucracy of which he was a part. But the banality of his evil deeds shows to Arendt not only bad judgment but a complete lack of thought as well, an apparent incapacity even to perceive the importance of asking basic questions about the meaning of what he and his government were effecting. He had, in Arendt's interpretation, functional common sense and a true grasp of the facts of his work: He knew what he was doing and those to whom he was doing it, but he did not give meaning to what he did, much less to his life. Had he thought well about it, he would have begun with largely meaningless activity and meaninglessness in his life.

Arendt's distinction between truth, the product of careful intellection, and meaning, and hence her distinction between intellect and thought, comes to bear on disciplined knowledge no less than on people who carry out evil deeds. Scientists and intellectuals, in spite of knowing many truths, often conceive violently foolish policies because they do not think about the meaning that their policies could have or about the meaning that could enhance the values on which the policies are based. They do not consider the reasons that constitute their own convictions, or the assumptions that are invested in their recognitions.[2]

The meaninglessness of solely intellectual grasp and organization and that of accepted beliefs and values makes us think. Why?

Arendt finds several reasons. The most prominent one is that the human mind comprises an inherent interest in meaning. It is "a natural need of human life" (191). She says that mentation enjoys a basic unity that inclines its various functions to move toward meaningful synthesis, that is, toward thinking (13, 57–58). In this context she can say that each person has a given responsibility to think, that all people *should* give attentive consideration to whatever they do and experience. We are made to think in the absence of meaning because a natural interest in meaning is constitutive of our makeup. The mind loves meaning in meaning's absence; that is, for Arendt, the human mind composes a natural desire for meaning.

A second reason Arendt gives for our having to think is found in the possible interconnection of thought and action. In an important sense, to

2. See, for example, Arendt's *On Violence* (San Diego: Harcourt Brace, 1969) in which she addresses especially the thoughtlessness and hence meaninglessness of the disciplines. In addition to raising consciousness concerning the lack of meaning in many conceptions of scientific truths and methods of prediction, she wants also to spur political theorists to think about violence, a largely ignored topic, in order to see more clearly what many political theories mean. See also *LM*, 5.

think is, as she says, an event of natality, a birth of meaning, a coming to life, that at best leads to a second natality of word and deed—that is, to social and political engagements (204).[3] These natalities make human selves —give rise to them—as distinct to social robots of common sense and unconsidered knowledge. "To think is to be *fully* alive," she says (178, emphasis added). And her repeated conviction is that our native interest in happiness, harmony, virtue—our native interest in a good life—makes us think, and not only to think but also to speak and act in the world. It's not thinking that makes us speak and act. It's our interest, especially when we think about it, in having meaningful social and political lives. The life of the mind is not made for banality. It is made for the fulfillment of its given drive for active and meaningful unity, and although she does not say so specifically as far as I know, she means too, I believe, that the mind's full life finds its satisfaction in a second birth that departs from thought and occurs through passionate citizenship. Thinking—the very meaning of thinking—suggests strongly, although it does not require, that the thinker engage the world as a social activist (184–85). That is a suggestion that I assume Arendt knew herself to follow as she wrote her books as well as when she engaged in other activities of citizenship. At least I can report that I experience her writing as a performance of that meaningful self-knowledge.[4]

I note at this point that what makes us think according to Arendt is a definitive intentionality of mind that has degrees of fulfillment in connection with a fundamental and a priori unity. Insofar as she distinguishes sharply between thinking and palpable social and political judgment and action—I will say more about this distinction—Arendt does not interpret thinking or its intentions with the thorough historicity and intrinsic social and political composition that a well-developed account of being in the world requires. My observation in passing is that her appropriation of Plato, Aristotle, and Kant, in addition to her profound suspicion of Heidegger's conception of dasein, stand in the way of that worldliness of thinking that at times she probably wanted.[5] Had she not thought of thinking in terms of a given, intentional, and to an important extent self-generating subjective

---

3. See also Arendt's *The Human Condition* (Chicago: University of Chicago Press, 1957), 176–81.

4. Citizens are concerned, by definition, with the world around them. To understand the meaning of the concept "citizen" is to understand the importance of concerned, thoughtful engagement with whatever is going on—to "examine" what is said and done (182). "Consciousness" is not synonymous with thinking, for Arendt, but thinking is nonetheless conscious and finds irreplaceable satisfaction, I believe she thinks, in appearances of responsible social consciousness, that is, in citizenship (183).

5. I base this observation primarily on Arendt's several discussions of Plato, Aristotle, and Kant vis-à-vis thinking in *LM,* part 1, "Thinking."

life, however, she would have lost the kind of imperative that she wanted (185). She wanted to show that autonomy of thought produces meaning—makes meaning—and at best looks beyond itself and finds a culmination in commonsense activity and intelligent knowledge. We can find in the mind's undispersed and unworldly autonomy the definitive standards for such activity and knowledge.

Arendt calls the "infrastructure, as it were" of the mind's questing and always incomplete unity our finitude (201). Human finitude arises, as far as thinking is concerned, in mental activity itself when we consider such activity solely on its own terms. Thought composes its own "time sensation." She calls it "the time sensation of the thinking ego," an "inner state of which we are aware when we have withdrawn from the appearances and find our mental activities recoiling characteristically upon themselves" (202). This sensation originates in the thinking ego's enactment. The occurrence of the thinking ego is "where" inner time sensation is located. We could call thinking a dwelling place of finitude or finitude's ethos. The inner time sensation is differentiated into experiences of past, present, and future in the very span of life between birth and death. Birth-death define, as it were, each living and thoughtful moment. Birthing-dying are ceaseless in the broken and discontinuous span of a life. To be present is to have lost presence in coming to be now, passing already, always already away, spanning in and toward not now. As alive we are present in the immanence, not of an archetypal or transcendental nature, but in the immanence of the stretch of birth-death. It is an immanence of a "continuously flowing stream of sheer change" (203). Such flow streams in thinking as well as in nonreflective life. So we have in the mind both a dimension of self-generating autonomy with its intention of unification and a process of continuous change and differentiation that makes definitive and timeless identity impossible.

Thinking, Arendt says, must always begin afresh as it searches for meaning (178). "[W]hat was meaningful while you were thinking dissolves the moment you want to apply it to everyday living" (196). "What thinking actualizes in its unending process is difference" (187). Its individuated achievements and realizations are subject to eradication as well as to constant, temporal change and must be rethought, repeated anew, if they are to continue. When we connect these descriptive claims to her observation that life without thought "is not merely meaningless, it is not fully alive," we see that our lives are fulfilled in a budding and dehiscence of meaning that comes to pass without perfection, clear applicability, or substantial durability (191). Thinking is "the dematerialized quintessence of being alive," and it happens with the limitations of natality, ending, and broken completions. It's no wonder that Arendt calls thinking dangerous (176). Its own eventuation comprises alertness to the indifference of its "infrastructure" before the finest accomplishments of insight, recognition, creation, and under-standing. The finitude of thinking composes a merciless neutrality that re-quires of thinking what Arendt names its homelessness, its lack of fit with sensation and worldly interaction—its "out of order activity." "Thinking always deals with absences and removes itself from what is present and close at hand" (199). This expresses, I believe, the intense alienation that Arendt finds in the eventuation of thoughtful human life. In its meanings, thought inevitably effects the loss of a sense of reality—unless it is supplemented by an altogether different sensibility, that of belonging in the social commu-nality of a group. And with such belonging, of course, comes not only the opportunities of citizenship but also the convenience of common sense, heedless certainties, and, above all, banality.

Although Arendt sometimes observes that thinking is limited in its ref-erences to distillations, mental constructs, and invisible essences, human finitude for her is not limited to those things. And although she indicates that language and the loss of continuity in our *geistige* tradition give philos-ophers the most to think about, there is an important sense in which the *happening* of thought and meaning, and not only language about them, can make thought think some of its most important questions. The word *fini-tude* when it is applied to thinking names an indifferent temporal inevita-bility that is the same as thinking's occurrence. I doubt that Arendt would be entirely satisfied with that sentence—where is the ego, then?—but I be-lieve it is one to which an important aspect of her descriptions of thinking leads us: The indifference of finitude describes the event of thought's life.

Arendt describes thinking with such words as examining, dissolving (e.g., of positive and negative concepts, 179), actualizing, interacting (with oneself, 191), dialoging, dealing (with absences, e.g., 199), generalizing, freeing us from frozen concepts, and analyzing. Usually, in keeping with these verbs, her thinking is representational and reportorial. But there is another dimension in her thought that is not the same as action by an ego and that is more appropriate to the indifference of finitude. We considered one instance of this dimension earlier when considering her account of thinking's sense of time that comes with its own happening. Even though her account of this sense is far from Heidegger's, given her thinking in the polarity of inner-outer, her location of time's sense in an ego, and her divi-sion of mentation according to faculties, she nonetheless indirectly intensi-fies alertness to a dimension of thought's occurrence that is neither active nor passive in its occurrence. She carries out this indirection by her focus on broken continuities. Broken continuities are definitive of the presence of thinking's Western lineage, and they are definitive of thinking's connection with both cognition and the social world. She emphasizes difference and differencing and does not emphasize stable identities. Her characteristic preoccupation with active citizenship bears witness to the indifference of finite happening, indifference to such values as justice, peace, and happiness. In the face of such indifference, people are called to find and defend what is valuable to them. This preoccupation attests to the requirements of thoughtful vigilance and proactive social engagement, requirements that appear to be intrinsic to finite occurrence and that comprise the reign of breakage, eradication, indeterminacy, and unpredictability with all meanings and values. Arendt's thought knows itself to be limited by thoughtlessness and mere absence of meaning. We find in her work considerably more than its claims and convictions; we find directly manifest a vigilance that finite life requires. We also find by indirection the dimensions of finitude, dimensions that dissolve in our representations of them. They will not appear directly as re-presentations. These are dimensions that need, I believe, a manner of thinking that is different from Arendt's, one that provides a different sensibility, a different life and valence, in its expression of finite life's thoughtful occurrence. It would be thinking *of* finite life, in a subjective-genitive sense, and not thinking only *about* finite life.

Arendt's sense of the nonrepresentable dimension of thinking, however, does come to expression when she writes that the only adequate metaphor for thinking is "the sensation of being alive . . . all questions concerning the aim or purpose of thinking are as unanswerable as questions about the aim or purpose of life" (197). I do not think that there is an adequate metaphor for thinking (or for being alive, for that matter), and I do think that the idea of adequation is inappropriate in the context of metaphors and living events; but I appreciate Arendt's sense that when we speak about the life of thinking—its ethos—we are always at a remove from the addressed. "Thinking always deals with absences," as we have seen (199). And Arendt's thought in its struggle, impatience, sense of danger, and continuous process of beginning again and again thinks of, and not only thinks about (perhaps more than she knew), a dimension that while given to self-showing is not subject to either truth, as Arendt defines it, or meaning.

HEIDEGGER: *WAS HEIßT DENKEN?*

Arendt's epigraph for the first section of *The Life of the Mind* is a quotation from Heidegger that ends with the line "thinking does not endow us directly with the power to act." She agrees with that sentence, and her agreement figures a serious problem for her. The gap between thinking and judgment and that between thinking and responsible action in the world define a vacuity that makes possible meaningless evil on the part of thoughtless activists and meaningless lack of good sense on the part of thinkers. But she hopes that "the habit of examining [i.e., thinking about] whatever happens to come to pass or to attract attention regardless of results and specific content" might be "one of the conditions that makes man abstain from evildoing or even actually 'condition' them against it" (*LM*, 5).

That hope, with a resonance and emphasis that set her work apart from Heidegger's, is informed by a belief that careful thought can add positively and incommensurably to policy formations and direction as well as to intelligent activity in the world. Thoughtful consideration of situations surely contributes an important measure of care and deliberation to attitudes and practical actions, but such considerations are, as Arendt says, composed of analysis, dealing, generalizing, dialoging, discussion, and argumentation—they compose various kinds of representation on the part of intelligent subjects.

We have seen that according to Arendt thought produces meaning as a result of its analyses and evaluations. This production is not simply a representing activity but one that initiates something new in connection with perceptions and intellection: the creation not of truth but of purpose, reasons for carrying on in some ways and not others, the intensification that comes with marked significance, and an enlarged as well as detailed sense for consequence and implication. The productivity of thinking is found in the interested work of a transcendental, representing ego. In her preoccupation with representational activity and a drawing transcendental unity, does Arendt attend to the uninterested and indifferent *occurrence* of thinking? Is she alert to the *occurrence* of its limited timeliness as she analyzes its productive penchant for unifying meanings?[6]

With this question we turn to Heidegger. He is remarkably persistent as he limits and puts into question traditional conceptions of thought and reconsiders the force of subjectivity in thinking. An option to thought as representation or ego-centered production emerges in it. In his thinking we engage an ethos, a way of living with the life of thought as well as with things in the world. Does he return us to contemplation as a haven outside of political disturbance and beyond ethical implication? We will have to see.

A first step toward thinking, Heidegger says, takes place when we "dispose everything [we do] so that what we do answers [appropriately] to

---

6. When we think, as she interprets thinking, we consider ideas and essences, desensualized, and disembodied entities in an important removal from palpable occurrences. I find no hint in her work that in thinking psychological and cultural histories come to bear in the very texture of its weave, that blood, neurons, and chemicals are intimately involved in the thinking process, that we think *with* things in *their* occurrences, that we engage events that engage us *in* thoughtful interchange, or that thought has much to do with lives that are not ideas. Yet Arendt speaks of the life of the mind and of thinking!

whatever addresses us as essential."[7] Thinking addresses not abstract essences but things in the midst of which we live (371). Thought begins in the world with what lives, and at best intensifies people's affirmative connection with the lives, the very being of things. The thinker's opportunity is "to make everything we do answer to whatever addresses itself to us as essential" (373). That means that as we think we let ourselves enter into questions that engage what no inventiveness can solve, and it means that, far from taking over another life, we allow lives to show themselves in the differences of their events as well as in the sameness of their eventuation (374).

Heidegger began to rethink *Being and Time* during the 1930s, especially in *On the Essence of Truth, Contributions to Philosophy,* and his work on Hölderlin. He brought these reconsiderations to bear on the question of thinking especially in the 1950s. In this process he reconsidered mortal temporality (as he had described it in *Being and Time*) in terms of the withdrawal of being. Being, the happening of whatever happens, in its withdrawal—in its mortal temporality—does not allow its being grasped as an acting agency or as a re-presentation.[8] It does not occur as an object or an acting subject or as any specific actuality. Being is not *a* difference from other beings. It happens rather more like a withdrawal . . . of being in the presencing occurrence of whatever appears to happen. "The event of withdrawal could be what is most present throughout the present" (374). A present occurrence lacks that sufficiency of being to fulfill a future without question. In the event of being's withdrawal the future is always in question, the past, always flowing away, and that intrinsic and quite nonintellectual questionability defines a present happening; it composes a factor of always ending. This factor is not due to anything people do or can do. It is the factor of being's withdrawal which, in its draft, leaves opening, question, possibility, need, a power of insufficiency, and mortal determination: Being's withdrawal, in its draft, leaves finite lives with the question of their continuing to be; the draft of being's withdrawal leaves the question of being. And, of course, the question of time.

---

7. Martin Heidegger, "What Calls for Thinking?" in *Basic Writings,* trans. David Farrell Krell (San Francisco: HarperSanFrancisco, 1993), 370. Unless otherwise noted, parenthetical page numbers in this section refer to this essay.

8. Arendt's reflections on natality in thinking arise, as we have seen, in the context of transcendental unity that comes to expression in human beings' predisposition to unifying meaning. Meaning emerges in the draw of such unity. In the absence of transcendental presence, on the other hand, Heidegger finds beginnings in the withdrawal of being. As transcendental grounding drops out of his thought, another beginning for thought emerges, one that does not indicate a grounded predisposition in thought founded on presence, but one born of loss of being, "another beginning" in the language of his *Beiträge zur Philosophie.*

"Our essential being bears the stamp of that draft," Heidegger says. Our own living eventuation "points toward it" (374). Our lives are drafted in their happening, occurring, as they do, in the strange perpetuation of presencing with loss of presence. Our eventuation happens as spatial and temporal limitation, and, like Heidegger says of being, our happening, our mortal lives, do not take place as objects or subjects or as a represented figure. Our occurrence slips away from such structures and compositions, withdraws quite palpably in a living draft of being different before the posited constancy of intellectual essences and reasonably fixed identities. Whoever we are to whomever, our lives already were and are in withdrawal. An identity is never the last word. Nor is a meaning.

Heidegger proposes that we consider thinking as a kind of historical disposition that arises with alertness in its own temporal occurrence and with alertness in the occurring of whatever happens and shows itself, that is, alertness to the life of whatever composes our phenomenal environment. This would be not quite a habit but a disposition that provides a temperament that is inclined toward the eventuation of things and not primarily toward *what* or *who* they are; that's important—*who* or *what* they are—but another matter. We are speaking now of positive inclination—a temperament or disposition—that, in the *draft* of being's withdrawal, disposes itself of figurations of fixation and certainty and pays attention to the ways different lives, in their living, happen in their self-showing differences—and pays attention as well to the ways we can address these differences so that their lives and their manner of difference might stand out in our address. Such words that Heidegger uses as allow, let be, dispose, address, appropriate, profess, affirm—these words describe a way of life that he names "thinking," an ethos of finitude in which the ways mortal, transient, and elusive lives happen require of thought a considerable jump outside of our usual manners of identification or reflection.

If we grant that Heidegger is accurate in his description of what he names thinking, we, and he in his accuracy, are nonetheless at a considerable remove from what we are talking about. Our descriptive language, whether accurate or not, needs to direct us beyond its meaning and to thinking's occurrence. Even the conception of finitude needs, in its limitations, reconsideration in the draft of thinking's own event. So let me take another approach to the ethos of finitude. Perhaps the lapse at this moment of transition will allow a thought that a continuity of address would make more difficult. I feel as though I face a situation like those engaged by musicians, especially in situations of improvisation when instruments or voices answer each other, one building on the other with a difference that hears and answers the other, whether in dissonance or harmony or both in variation, hears and answers with an intermediacy that is not just the sum of those in exchange, but a third event, something of its own.

As an interlude and with the thought of finitude in a context of withdrawal I invite you to imagine the time of your dying, a time when the importance of your past accomplishments fades and the events of your life appear past with little or no future prospect. I am imagining—prospecting, you could say—a time in which the loss of presence that comes with the presence of memory is especially pronounced and poignant. I am (you are) about to cease, in this case with alert sensibility. If your mortal reverie is like mine, in the withdrawal of connections and remembered experiences, in the strange and immediate expectation of complete loss, the withdrawn presence of the remembered carries a considerable draw. With the letting go that can accompany the experience of dying I find myself—oh happy serenity should my dying happen this way!—in the draw of the loves and the love of my life, of moments of beauty, of the lives of my children and grandchildren, of self-forming feelings and experiences. They happen like a vortex of precious things. What then happens in memory happens with the force not only of loss and letting go but also of a draw toward the remembered. Withdrawals, letting go, and being drawn, all at once.

Now, in my present and living reverie of the time of my dying, I also find accentuation of the withdrawing present, of the passage of things, of all present things including their immediacy with me and mine with them. In my projection of my dying their lives stand out as they come to pass, and I in their intensified wake feel a draw to their continuing to come to pass, a sense of the importance of their happening. The wakefulness of *their* passage, if I may put it this way, composes a draw to a special alertness. I expect that Heidegger is right to think that, in his terminology, the question of being, when it is intensified with specific alertness, can engender a sensibility that prizes the happening, the lives of things. This is a sensibility born in being's withdrawal and in that remarkable opening, occasioned by the withdrawal, of a space for passing and self-showing lives. I expect too that thinking might take place in such alertness, not entirely unlike the alertness addressed in the rather more stark imagery of coming to my death.

This imaginative play, of course, does not constitute what Heidegger had in mind by "thinking." But when we consider the withdrawal of lives in the ordinance of time and with reference to Heidegger's thought, we are considering the ungraspable happening of the difference of being, being's never coming fully to presence, and its Mnemosynic quality of coming forth by flowing back toward what can never come fully to be. Our imaginative moment projected into a future and in that projected future remembered backward as it were. It projected beyond our present moment of reverie and toward losses yet to come. We then moved back from the time of our dying to the present dying of our time. We remembered in an odd way one of the oddest dimensions of our lives: the withdrawal of being in its coming to pass, the dying of lives in their living. My dying, your dying now, here, in this breath. The withdrawal of being.

If thinking *about* being is not a necessary condition for what Heidegger has in mind in his account of thought, however, thinking *about* being's withdrawal can nonetheless help in providing a threshold for a different thinking. At the moment we are reaching for the eventuation of what Heidegger calls thinking. "To call (*heißen*)," he says, "means to speak to something by addressing it." "Accordingly, when we ask the question, 'what is calling us to thinking?' in the sense that it asks, 'what is it that claims us so that we must think?' we then are asking: 'What is it that enjoins our essential being to think, and thus lets it arrive in thinking there to shelter it?'" (388). Presumably, as we come into the area where his thought takes place, we can develop a sense for what he calls thinking and also undergo the call to thought of which he speaks.

I am attempting to call attention to the life, the eventuation, of Heidegger's thought: In his language, I am attempting to let his address, by its happening, point to the addressed. Or at least I am attempting to make evident that that's what we need to do on his terms when we think with his language of the call to thinking in the withdrawal of being. The lives of the living slip our grasp. Even the life of our thought slips our grasp. The larger observation—a self-limiting observation—is that when we think something with alertness, we let its life show itself as it appears. This letting-be aspect of thought not only lets something show itself as itself. It also lets thinking— its own event—be as *it* shows *itself.* Thinking occurs, in Heidegger's language, as essentially an enjoining event, and "essentially" means in this context that thinking composes a release that shows its life in the releasing. That is, "essentially" in this context means enjoining being's withdrawal and the occurrence of whatever happens in the mortal space of withdrawal.

A remarkable dimension of releasing can be apparent when we imagine ourselves dying. There is a considerable alteration in the way we care, for example. Dying, we care for our dying mostly. In the happy instance I described, we let ourselves die, yielding to the advance of memories' losses and to the approaching end to our possibility and futurity. We find an accord with our dying in our dying. We might care enormously for those we are leaving, but we care-in-leaving, and the difference of their lives can stand out in intense relief. On such occasions, their differences, their own lives, their being there as they are could well stand out as wonderful, as, just so, yes, that is you. Or they could stand out otherwise. If your imaginative play is like mine, or if you have been close to death with alertness and with time to feel yourself dying, you have found, perhaps, that many things appear in intense relief in their lives—the room, a plant, an animal, as well as certain people—many things. Our possessions also can appear largely in the disposition of dispossession. So much is marked by a process of stark disjunction. We, dying, enjoin the disjunction, not unlike thinking in alertness to groundlessness in the draw of being's withdrawal.

I would like to highlight two aspects of release and withdrawal. First, in such release the lives of things trump the utility of things and people, and trump as well our need to grasp things and hold them, as it were, in disembodied, operational definitions. There is nothing intrinsically wrong with grasping and operating with definitions—those activities are required by our needs and limitations. But there is a noteworthy difference in the ethos of what Heidegger calls thinking and its disposition toward release and that of a disposition to define and use.

The second aspect of release and withdrawal that I want to highlight is found in their composition of the eventuation of our lives. Heiddegger's descriptive claim is that what we might call finitude and what he calls the withdrawal of being addresses the very happening of people's lives. He finds human lives disclosed and apparent in being's coming to pass. In his language we can say that being's withdrawal happens essentially; it happens as living and not as disembodied essence.

So we are called to think by the happening of our lives, by living always in being's coming to pass. The ethos of release describes the living occurrence of relations in the world. This ethos also describes thinking as Heidegger finds it and haltingly carries it out. In the life of thinking the happening of whatever happens apparently shines out. The happening of whatever happens embodies a call. It is a call to let the happening happen, to let it compose its own evidence. And this dimension of happening also composes, according to Heidegger, a call to thought, a call to the alertness in self-showing connections that Heidegger names thinking. It is a call that happens intrinsically in people's being in the world.

Is it not remarkable that what calls for thinking occurs in the phenomenal quality of things, in their self-showing?[9] This call, as Heidegger accounts it, happens intrinsically in people's being in the world, in a nonreducible interactivity of beings. To "own" something, to belong with something essentially and to appropriate it (for Heidegger) is to be in nonconceptual engagement with it in a context of interconnections. Such belonging is to let a life happen as it takes place disclosively in its context. The infinitives, to own and to release, each intend the other, and their essential

---

9. *Verhältnis* is one of his technical terms for such interconnectedness.

dimension in our lives is part and parcel of being's withdrawal. In other words, release and withdrawal with the entire compass of finite occurrence are entirely neutral as far as their application is concerned. They mean nothing other than their own occurrence.

To turn release into an imperative is to insert into it too much of a sense of consciousness and a tendency toward a traditional conception of conscience. That would be like the kind of conception that turned Heidegger away from the language and limits of *Being and Time*. Release and being's withdrawal occur without consciousness, although they indifferently, that is, without consciousness or subjective interest, happen as dimensions of conscious life. The *occurrence* of lives, the occurrence of caring, the occurrence of coming to pass—being happens indifferently in such occurrences vis-à-vis the values by which we distinguish ourselves and our social environments. Being's withdrawal as it is released in thinking has neither place nor countenance. Like classical beauty, it occurs only in its drawing withdrawal. And "being" names the happening of our lives. As we live "we" belong with being as—to use language that Heidegger uses but with an irony that I believe he does not intend—we belong with being as our closest neighbor, closest in its indifferent happening no matter how distant that indifference seems to the content of our thought from the content of our preoccupations.

Arendt and Heidegger agree in this, that a necessary bridge between thinking and social activity does not exist in an a priori region of composition. In the language of this chapter, indifference is found in the withdrawal of continuity among present occurrences. Such absence of necessary connection befits finite lives. But tensions are apparent among dispositions of release and those of passions and grasp. This is not a tension of either/or's but one of emphasis, shade, and inclination. Arendt and Heidegger also agree in finding question and loss of meaning intrinsic to the situation that calls for thought and that describes thinking. Social and political activity, on the other hand, seems to require rather more certainty, at least in times of action, and to be helped by questionability only if questioning is strategically valuable; working passionately in social causes makes us people of faith, if only momentarily. Both are surely right: In the indifference of being there is no necessary connection between thought and the power to act.

Do we not need to let go of such agreements between Arendt and Heidegger, however, if we are to address the lives—the ethos—of their thinking, let go of agreeing and disagreeing as well if we are to undergo the ways their thinking dwells with things? Such dwelling appears outside of the circumference of agreement. Thoughtful address and hearing seem indifferent to whether we take hold of things in the same way. This manner of thinking is a way of dwelling that finds freedom from argumentation, refutation, and the many forceful actions of representative mentation, actions that are moved by commitments to hierarchies of value and meaning. Is not thinking's indifferent release of that contesting manner of perception its—thinking's—particular genius, that it hears and answers in a dimension of questionable, virtually meaningless freedom from the forces of value-oriented separation?

I do not want to suggest that thought is purely indifferent, that it is fully released from drives and desires that have in their wake the dreary histories of unending conflicts. Thought not composed of historical and social histories? Thought without the histories of given bodies, without the indifferent work of cellular organizations? Thought without identity? Purely indifferent thought? No, I don't think so. But the physicality, historicity, and identity of thinking are other issues for another time. For now the question is a limited one of the indifference of differential happenings, an indifference that seems important for Arendt's recognitions of "the sensation of being alive," of essences, and of the intellect's lack of aim and purpose. The indifference of being's withdrawal as Heidegger finds it seems compositional not only in the release of beings in thinking but also in the happening of what calls for thinking. I expect that a sense of such indifference is invested in most of Western reflective endeavor, that it hovers over and haunts many of the figures of Western hope. I expect too that the thought of indifference promises an important growth of alertness. This would be a growth of limitation on those projections of values and identities that make the occurrence of life to seem to care, and to care especially for a "we," to commission "us" to make the world into an instrument of our intentions. This would be an awareness, for example, that arises from the life of what Heidegger calls thinking, arises from the equivalence, the *Gleichgewicht,* the indifference of this life. It would be an awareness of an odd kinship in life's happening that is not measurable by identities or meanings.

Does such growth in the thought of finitude promise a better world to live in? Yes, in ways similar to the difference that experiences of beauty make; like the differences that perceptive and open regard for lives make; like the differences that release from the forces of instrumental obsession and desire for conquest and control make; like the differences that freedom from the hooks of power and its attendant need to be right make. But people who know of such release can nonetheless carry out cultural and psychological trajectories that effect seemingly needless loss and suffering. Such release is no guarantee of justice or transcendence of practices that are recognized in other contexts as harmful to people. In finite dwelling places there are no timeless answers, and we are forced always—finitude's always—to fall back on commitments and on inherited values and forms of perception that figure limitation and very likely pain and heedless losses.

Does knowing such things make a difference? Of course it does, but even if such knowledge could compose a wisdom it would be, wouldn't it, wisdom in the wake of being's withdrawal? A wisdom of knowing that for now the gaps between thinking and action as well as those between thoughts figure a dying release, figure finitude's manner of dwelling? In this abode we know that there are only small accuracies, that accuracy is not the goal of this thinking, and that a certain carelessness lets thinking be thinking. Do not the question marks of these final paragraphs write rather more of finitude's life than the declarative sentences that precede them? Or, more likely, that last question is a mere conceit. It's *needing* to order that's important, isn't it—in this case needing to order words and sentences? And it's the lack of order that ordering makes apparent—that is what shows finitude, isn't it? Especially the order of declarative sentences? And silences? As declarative order finishes and tumbles, it seems, over edges that make no declaration, silences show more than can be declared, show nothing to agree on—perhaps something like dying and natality at once. Isn't that where finite thought finds its home?

FIVE

Another Look at "Soul":
Mimetic Geist

The whole frame of things preaches indifference.
—R. W. Emerson

WHAT PASCAL LACKED

Pascal had a monstrous intellectual conscience, according to Nietzsche; but he did not have what it takes to figure out and determine the history of Western religious sensibility (*Beyond Good and Evil,* section 45). Though admirable in its monstrosity, Pascal's intellectual conscience was not made for "the great hunt," for the pursuit of what has happened and is carried in the formation of Western religious awareness and passion. The subject for such a hunt would be an exceptional agency of recognition, naming, affection, and evaluation. The subject that is pursued—Western spirituality—is active in the pursuit: The pursuer is to a degree—a self-endangering degree—the pursued, and the direction is toward a fundamental transformation of not only our recognition of the way Western religious and ethical sensibility began and developed but also and at once the way the recognizing pursuer's awareness began and developed. The danger of major transformation and destruction inheres in the knower as well as in the known.

A conscience different from Pascal's is at issue, one that is no less monstrous but much more devilish, distant, playful, and malicious, a Dionysian conscience that takes delight in its own undergoing and self-overcoming. A sensibility that is Dionysian figures something vastly different from Pascal's. This sensibility is no less sacrificial, no less wounded than Pascal's, but it is without hope for divine promise and presence: The life of Dionysus is at best a mask of gods' (or God's) death and absence. The sensibility is Dionysian (given to self-overcoming *in* its own identity) in part because its

own agency is problematic in the pursuit of the problem of religious sensibility, in part because salvation and forgiveness are not at stake, and in part
because it dissolves in the force of representation and occurs as a strange
mimesis of—virtually an art of—voided presence: a mimesis with no identity to imitate. While Pascal's intellect had with it much that is Dionysian,
he, in common with Western spiritual agency, didn't *know* it and thus did-
n't know to cultivate it or how to suffer it creatively.

The sensibility of the pursuit is also characterized by a dangerous divi-
sion: The intention of the pursuit is at cross-purposes with itself. The predisposition toward the pursuit and toward thorough knowledge of spiritual
life was forged in the process that produced religious awareness and conscience in Western civilization. The pursuer, after all, has a conscience, even
a bad conscience that can understand—more than understand, *know*—Pascal's sense of sin and fall from grace. It is also a conscience that feels badly
about that kinship with Pascal's conscience. A dimension of the pursuer's
conscience wants betterment, is drawn to sickness, and has a sense for awful
divine presence. This sensibility also has another dimension, something like
a perspective on its own ethos of religious evaluation and on its own formation that gives goods and bads, divines and evils to appear with the force of
identities. This dimension constitutes a perspective that enjoys an indifferent disposition, a liberty of heedlessness, something like freedom from bias
before goods and evils, a dimension of unconcern that allows the concern
in doing a history of Western religious sensibility a range of freedom and a
quality of transformative force unavailable to the disposition in question. I
refer to the indifference that characterizes "that vaulting heaven of bright,
malicious spirituality that would be capable of surveying from above, arranging and forcing into formulas this swarm of dangerous and painful experiences" (*BGE*, section 45).

"That vaulting heaven of bright, malicious *spirituality*"? What does
Nietzsche have in mind by *Geistigkeit*? Certainly a state of mind that is at
once historical in its formation and ahistorical in its eventuation. The word
suggests "the human soul," a dimension of inner experience as well as *spir-
itus, anima mens,* and *genius.* Something that is lively and aware, coming to
pass, a region with limits, reach, and dimension, with depth, height, and
surface, as it were. *Geistigkeit* can connote multiple identities, none of which
defines "it." *Geistigkeit* can mean a harbor and a producer of freedom, a site
of potential pride and self-confidence as well as of enslavement, self-mock-
ery, and self-mutilation. Western *Geistigkeit* is figured by subjection and
dominance, beauty and ugliness, comprehension, foolishness—it names a
full range of conscious achievement, failure, and ability.

The aspect of *Geistigkeit* that I want to consider comes to bear in the
free spirit (*der freie Geist*). In *Beyond Good and Evil* Nietzsche gave an ac-

count of this kind of spirituality prior to his observations on the religious way of being from which I quoted above. The account of the free spirit maps a departure and articulates an agency for departure from the traditional prejudices embedded in Western spiritual achievement. In this process his writing embodies not only the common lineage that he shares with Pascal but also a kind of spirituality that Pascal could not bring to creative expression. The aspect of spiritual indifference, one that produces differences in a context of overcoming its own formation, points out indirectly a weakness in many forms of Western spiritual life as well as in Pascal's. It is a weakness that expresses a desire for something personal, even humanlike, at the outer borders of spiritual agency, something that saves us from the indifference that permeates living events. This is a dimension of indifference that figures nonetheless Pascal's sense of number and calculation, the agonizing distance of God, and the soul's implacable need for suffering and abnegation before the requirements of a possible salvation. Nietzsche's Pascal is like a half-waking Dionysus who embodies an only partially reflected sense that indifferent necessity permeates identities and gives them a backdrop and inevitability of oblivion and generation, and an inevitability that holds identity, birth, and death apart.

The high probability is that Western spiritual enactment carries with it much that follows Pythagorean and Dionysian experience. A certain neutrality often characterizes the lives of Western divinities in their distance and self-absorbed enactments. That is a neutrality that often appears to characterize spiritual freedom before whatever is deathly and time-limited. Such freedom can appear without care, that is, indifferently, in the force of its own enactment.

Perhaps we Westerners need to affirm such indifference if we wish to carry out a definitive aspect of our spiritual heritage. If we did affirm it, what and how would we affirm?

A TENSE BOW

Nietzsche speaks of Pascal's *intellectual* conscience. Recall that one of Pascal's major works has the title *L'Esprit géométrique: The Spirit of Geometry,* the *Geist* of geometry. In that work he *showed* the advantages of geometrical procedure in establishing reasonable claims of truth, given that no axioms are provable. And he showed in a second book, *De l'art de persuader,* that this art requires people to recognize the drastic limits of reason in the formation of reasonable knowledge. In yet a third book, *Experiences nouvelles touchant le vide,* he showed that contrary to the established scientific belief of the time, nature does indeed tolerate a vacuum. So far so good. Pascal was relentless in his critique of easy thought and ill-conceived beliefs as he showed that the source or sources of truth cannot be found in rational activity, and he was equally conscientious in showing that a full skepticism is not really possible for alert human beings. The spirit of the highest form of knowledge, according to Pascal, geometrical knowledge, is found in part in both its ideality and the severity of its limits. The art of the best persuasion carries out the knowledge that first principles are not provable, and we must bring people to experiences of nonrational intention and revelation if we are to find the real beginnings for the certainties that we affirm. And nature, he showed, far from being seamlessly filled with invisible matter, is characterized by empty space. Merely space. Indifferent to any possible content.

Such careful, impassioned intellectual work on the limits of the intellect and the probability of space without presence, I assume, won Nietzsche's admiration, even if Pascal was insensitive to the historical development of spirit and its value. Pascal also recognized the profound degree of human spiritual suffering and unhappiness—the misery that comes with Western human life in its conflicted uncertainty and mortality. And all of these intellectual accomplishments are unified by two further impassioned claims: People need to hear God, and the only true aid to such hearing is faith in Jesus Christ. Pascal's spirit, so close and so far from a freedom available to it, ending with a calculation of the risks of not believing in the Christian God, developing an art of religious persuasion based on fear and a desire for eternal happiness, filling the vacuum of ignorance and limitation with a horror of unredeemed life and death and, in that horror, with an image of enduring divine, if hidden, presence—Pascal is a figure of spiritual tension between recognized, mortal limitation and a tradition-bound affirmation of figures of eternity. It's clearly an art, Pascal's thought, but an art without acceptance of its own historical development or the indifference that gives art to be: monstrous in the tension it composes at the heart of Pascal's sincerity and conscientious intelligence. His spirit forms a fine image of its greater progenitor, Western spirituality—torn by an attempted affirmation of spiritual freedom in an art the content of which both affirms and denies it. Pascal's art assumes an awful, human freedom from God and Truth at the same time that it affirms God's necessity for that freedom.

Nietzsche writes of spiritual tension in his preface to *Beyond Good and Evil:* "But the fight against Plato or, to speak more clearly and for 'the people,' the fight against the Christian-ecclesiastical pressure of millennia . . . has created in Europe a magnificent tension of the spirit the like of which had never yet existed on earth: with so tense a bow we can now shoot for the most distant goals." This spiritual tension, he says, figures the "need of the spirit." The need is the stretch of Western spirit, its tautness, imbalance, and unrest. This tension composes the nurturance as well as the sickness of free spirit, and, as we shall see, it is a site of disposition without bias to the poles of the tension. This spiritual tension is without care except for its inclination to stretch to a breaking point. This observation suggests that the Western spiritual heritage has a definitive core of life that bends toward its own breaking and that, in the context of Nietzsche's thought, is severely mistaken when it gains the imagery of self-sacrifice in a context of divine reward. It is the threatening force of this tension so apparent in Pascal's spiritual accomplishment, and the failed effort of deviation from the tension in Pascal's faith, that merits him one of Nietzsche's most appreciative adjectives: monstrous.

The tense bow finds its affirmation in "the free spirit." By the adjective *free*, Nietzsche intends a quality of mind that in its passionately interested, critical, and constructive activity reflects a dimension of indifference to most of the images and signs that organized what people have traditionally affirmed as good, evil, and holy. This reflection includes an inscribed indifference to images of free spirits' own moral value. ("The overcoming of morality, in a certain sense even the self-overcoming of morality—let this be the name for that long secret work which has been saved up for the finest and most honest, also the most malicious, consciences of today, as living touchstones of the soul"; *BGE,* section 32.) Moments might well occur when free-spirited activity seems enough for all time, seems to fulfill a destiny in free endeavor considerably in excess of individual creativity. But proper fulfillment of Western free-spiritedness happens as people enjoy the pretense of completion while their work moves toward overturning the very identity of "the" free spirit. In this release from the value of so many goods and bads as well as from universality combined with identity, the "vaulting heaven of bright, malicious spirituality" comes to bear. ("[T]here are heights of the soul from which even tragedy ceases to look tragic"; *BGE,* section 26.) The free spirit is now able to arrange things and create formulas of association in the knowledge that "spirit" is a process of appearing and imaging in a force of neutrality that makes all the difference.

Let's look more closely at this differential neutrality in the imagery of Nietzsche's thought.

THE COMING OF IMAGES

In *The Birth of Tragedy* Nietzsche describes a thoroughgoing influence on Western culture in a preclassical Greek experience of forces of nature and their connection to artistic productivity. Their experience, once given mythical/artistic expression, comes to compose the very disposition of indifference—a prereflective experience of differential neutrality—that is such a significant dimension in Western spirituality as Nietzsche finds it. In *The*

Birth of Tragedy he collects the definitive experiences (for our topic) around the images of Apollo and Dionysus and a force of like-making, mimesis.

Apollo, the bringer of dreams, figures in *The Birth of Tragedy* not only as a maker of dreams but also as the shining—the manifesting, the appearing—of dreams. As the Shining One, Apollo suggests the appearing of something that is otherwise invisible in ordinary activity. The preoccupation with invisible reality that so thoroughly saturated Greek experience, both early and late, takes the form of Apollo, who gives invisible realities (past, present, and future) to shine, for example, in the darkness of sleep: Nothing but sleep is happening, and then, like a shot out of the dark, a dream appears that is free of the constraints of waking life and that radiates a sense of its own, making apparent in itself what is hidden outside of itself, an icon of particular force that must be attended to and interpreted carefully because of the power and importance of its appearance. Apollo is the figure of the shining of appearance, not the figure of its content. Like Hermes, the sense of Apollo in this context comes not in the message but in the *appearing* of an otherwise largely invisible reality: not the meaning so much as the shining, the appearing, the breaking in of what is not a matter of common sense. At this point I note the bright, lofty indifference of Apollo to whatever the reality might be, the difference his shining makes, and the striking force that this Greek experience attributes to such occurrences.

Dionysus gives nothing to shine. Chaotic, often indeterminate, deteriorative of forms and orders, and yet vaguely alive and compelling, this strange . . . —is it a grouping of force and nonforce? Something like negative power? A figure of contextualized chaos? Dionysus happens with elision, inessential disintegration, oblivion. Mere passing away. And yet in the experience of passing away, in the slippage and failure of form, Greek people, early and late, found a sense of closeness with vitality, almost by antiphrasis, a resignation proper to suffering mortality, an experience approximate to reconciliation with boundless indifference to whatever matters.

Nietzsche finds in the tension of these two kinds of . . . experiences? forces? lived signs? . . . these two figures of order and disorder a connection that gave beauty in the form of tragedy to the senseless absence of order and value in the higher and lower reaches of mortal occurrences. In this art senseless dimensions of sense shine beautifully through human success and failure. Beauty in this context does not abolish anything, certainly not darkness and chaotic fate. Beauty, rather, gives them to shine in a crosshatched, tension-filled, maddening glory of order and chaos that comes to pass with a draw that gives people to want to say yes.

"Mimesis" provides Hellenic context for these two figurations of differential forces. This word describes occurrences when likenesses happen, and it can thereby name a manner of linkage among various occurrences of inception, growth, and decline. On the surface, "Apollo" and "Dionysus" name nonhuman forces of generation and decay, but their many legends add a vast range of subtlety and variation to their qualities. Artworks, for example, are like the inception and progress of plants and animals, like the transformative growth and passage of things, insofar as some thing comes from some other thing, and a new thing happens and becomes its own, whether it be a vine, a goat, a boat, a statue, or a drama. "Mimesis" articulates happenings of likenesses—that boat is like this one, this group of words reminds us of those, the clash of form and disaster in this play is like that of struggling mortals. And: the emergence of the boat is like the emergence of a sculpted form. The force of bringing about likenesses makes the differences of similarity, kinship, reminder, imitation, memory, and recognition. It is not especially an ordering force per se—although order without mimesis is not conceivable—but rather one of connection even when the connections do not compose a unity and allow disorder to shine. "Mimesis" also names the kinship of various kinds of making, whether or not the "maker" is a person or something else. The anonymity of mimesis is now the focus, because the indifference of this force to the likenesses it allows is part of— or at least like—the vault of the free spirits' spirituality.

How is that so?

A VAULT OF MIMETIC INDIFFERENCE

Nietzsche established part of the contrast between the free spirit and Pascal by recognizing that Pascal's spirituality fell prey to what Nietzsche wanted to uncover by "the great hunt." The connection I would like to make is that between this process of recognition (the great hunt) and the lineage that Nietzsche sets out to describe, that of the operation of mimesis in the birth (and death) of tragedy. There is a likeness, a kinship, between the lineage and its recognition, and this connection includes mimetic indifference. Mimetic indifference composes forcefully the vault of spiritual life as Nietzsche accounts it.

If Nietzsche is accurate, *our* feeling the impact that Greek tragedy had on their experience of being alive requires, if even possible, a mammoth and mind-stretching exercise. What are the dimensions of contemporary experience that are like those of the Greeks, who were moved by tragic beauty to want to live in spite of certain suffering, injustice, destruction, and death? Their experience, as Nietzsche imagines it, was in the absence of a sense of foundational meaning for "life." The very process of the performed tragedy—its life—carries no sense of universal meaning or authorship of the world. There is an exhilarating kind of affirmation that possesses none of the unities that images of a singular God or ordered Law impose. The modern charge of "merely aesthetic" against this force of art and beauty comes to Nietzsche as a symptom of spiritual deterioration so profound as to demand from spirits of unusual alertness and resolve (not Pascal's) recognition of the deterioration's inception and formation. But what is the living basis for Nietzsche's images of Greek aesthetic experience? And why would he think (know?) that some gifted spirits could now see at least the outlines of realities in Western sensibility that, by the very obtuseness of that sensibility, are usually invisible? What is the living basis for the great hunt? Especially in the nihilistic age based in the death of a Greek art of tragic affirmation?

We could turn now to any of several genealogies begun by Nietzsche, those of the value of good or of conscience, for example, or of the death of God or depreciation of physical pleasure. But for our present purposes, let's keep mimesis, Apollo, and Dionysus before us to see how, in the forces and collections they figure, we can find a likeness between them and the malicious vaulting sky in Western spirituality. That likeness would be the basic referent we're looking for to show a way whereby Western spirituality composes a tension that intends its self-overcoming (a midway marker of which Nietzsche found in the art and suffering of Pascal). We would show as well a threshold for contemporary access to Greek, tragic affirmation. An indifferent gathering of likenesses among irreducible differences is our key.

Mimesis, the Greek word, can suggest a relation of dependence: one writer's dependence on another, for example. The word also carries an overtone of the intense attentiveness required by disciplined memory. It also may designate experiences in which a power is exerted that brings likeness and the intimacy of acquaintance that likeness allows. In the context of *The Birth of Tragedy* and Nietzsche's reading of certain aspects of Greek culture, "mimesis" also suggests similarity of images and processes of figured representation. "Mimesis" names a power of imaging and engagement that allows comparison, complex recognition, interdependence among differences, as well as differences among similarities. The power of mimesis (faceless, without identity) also functions now in the emergence of images as they happen with similarity and difference. Mimesis takes place, for example, in the formation and interaction of signs and symbols, in any thing's sense and recognition. And when attended to, mimesis lets us know that our sensible worlds—wherever there are connections of likes—are like works of art, even though no particular person or subject can rightly be named as their creator. Mimetic power, seemingly like that in Greek experience, continues today as constitutive of relational events and hence as intrinsic to occurrences of recognition. It is a force of likeness, no matter what happens to be alike. This kind of power is indifferent to consequences, purposes, and values, like a neutrality of relational force. It would be a primary *geistige* factor in recognizing Christ as savior, God as dead, and Pascal as monstrous.

As in other of Nietzsche's observations, one of his thoughts here is that powerful functions carry with them memories and embedded dispositions. Nonvoluntary mimetic occurrences, I have said, have in them memory of what some Greeks appear to have affirmed: Powers of connection and kinship among things (including images) show nothing of fundamental justice, singular identity, or purpose. Mimetic power is without preference among options. As the force of likeness, it is like a sheer vaulting heaven, invisible to those without eyes to see. This lack of identity in mimesis, reflected so well in some Greek drama, composes a vault above the comparatively low ceiling of Pascal's agonized efforts to form a hope that human limitations are juxtaposed with another dimension of revealed and beneficent reality. Affirmation of this lack of identity in the force of likeness is also the site of genesis for a different kind of conscience, one that intends in a traditional way to be honest but now with an honesty that it knows is like a work of art, a mimetic event that presents and re-presents in the unbiased disposition of the power of tragedy. This unbiased disposition (mimesis) is a kind of *Geistigkeit* for Nietzsche, not like a person, divine or human, but like nothing other than the happening of likenesses, likenesses that come to form and degenerate into other likenesses. This kind of *Geist* doesn't mean a thing. Imaging, likening, re-presenting, expressing, figuring—something like art—take place as people come to know things and see with all manner of connections, kinships, and differences. Recognitions happen in the indifferent forces of likeness with formation and disappearance: a vault of alert eventuation with no one there but formed and deformed likenesses. Something like real masks.

People can hear no resonance with human compassion in Greek tragedy, where art, the gift of mimesis, joins the forces figured by Apollo and Dionysus—a grand simulacrum of the fate of all individuals. Tragedy as a functioning form carries the loss of whatever meaning it might also possess—dispossesses such meaning in Dionysus's power—and leaves the questions: Is being alive worth the effort? With the loss of everything, can you live without the promise, even the hope, of restitution? Tragedy is a living memory of the possibility of what Nietzsche called a pessimism of strength, of "an intellectual predilection for the hard, gruesome, evil, problematic aspect of existence, prompted by well-being, by overflowing health, by the fullness of existence."[1] This kind of pessimism—before the possibility of

---

1. "Attempt at Self-criticism," in *The Birth of Tragedy,* trans. Walter Kaufmann (New York: Vintage, 1967), 17.

which Pascal's own monstrous and unhealthy spirit failed, and in the force of which begins the great hunt for recognition of Western spirituality's generation and decay—this kind of pessimism lies embedded in the occurrence of tragedy before it can be denied. Such denial seems to be peculiar to a spiritual flight from tragedy—*down* from tragedy, we might say, when we have the vaulting heaven in mind. This refusal of a manner of *geistige* life by a manner of *geistige* life composes a very powerful tension—a tension whose occurrence we can now say is memorial, a history-bearer, one that in its power moves toward a release of itself in new images, new configurations of force, new manners of living.

That release in the forms of new knowledge is, of course, one of Nietzsche's intentions. One aspect of the new knowledge is an account of the tensions that composes his Western *geistige* life. Both the account and the knowledge to which it contributes take multiple forms, many of which are not compatible or consistent with the others and that are indifferent to many customary connections of compatibility. We might follow this indifference to traditional connections as one way to the vaulting heaven. Or we could follow Nietzsche's style of breakage and interruption, his dismissal of sacred axioms, or his occasional accomplishment of laughter before the values that he most cherishes. Whatever the way, we can find in his work the vaulting differential of mimetic indifference in the tragic confluence of powers of formation and deformation.

Who cares whether likeness and difference are indifferently mimetic in their relations? Not many philosophers in this country, at least. We philosophers in the United States have found worthy causes to espouse, many "-ists" by which to identify ourselves, not to mention intellectual pieties, both religious and nonreligious. We are busy with our philosophical-ethical good deeds, optimistic in our pursuit of political efficacy and timeliness. Very likely some of our most trenchant, philosophical differences will be bridged by people joining good causes, whether on the left or right of the spectrum, as we look to make a difference in our society by dint of careful analyses and descriptions and by alignments with those who need our gifts—especially with those who might put our thought to work in agencies and committees. Perhaps political differences will replace distinctly philosophical differences as the axis for argument and differentiation, and Western philosophy in this country, not entirely alien to its medieval heritage, will take its cues from sources that are not philosophical. Proper espousal and belief (as though they were not *geistige* events), not new arts of expression, new principles of aesthetic order, might become the goal of thought —with little sense for a vast, largely invisible neutrality at the historical core of our sympathies and affiliations. No sense of fate. An optimism with little awareness of the forces that play in it.

One ingredient in such a state of mind might be the exercise of slight care in reading the tradition that, though formative of our powers to know and represent, seems largely past. Strong espousal requires the courage of convictions (not their relentless interrogation or suspension), a kind of sincerity and seriousness not found among the complacent. Such sincerity and seriousness are also not found on the edges of Nietzsche's noncomplacent thought where his mimetic art is most forceful. Nietzsche might be accurate in his description of the resources of creative alertness in Western culture: What is sometimes called with admirable ambiguity "spirit" in the West is formed in a tragic struggle of forces best designated by figures and not concepts, forces that engender likenesses and their rules of connection, and forces that are often expressed in tensed forms of self-refusal. Were he accurate, we could say that our good will in philosophy, our desire to work for good causes, would mask conflicted currents of spirit that defy all "-ists" and make probable that our endeavors are like a satyr play after tragedy, certainly a relief after so much hopelessness but captured by histories that we enact and cannot know outside of alert engagement with mimetic power.

Or perhaps Nietzsche is only half-right. Perhaps our desire for proper beliefs, our well-intentioned, humanitarian philosophies, and our likeness mediated by "-ists" now effect a sky-change, a cosmic shift in Western *Geistigkeit.* Far from blindly fulfilling a destiny of misaimed and tragic tension, we are now engaged in a Great Reconstruction, one that makes a vault of optimism, with mistakes, surely, but without a fateful tension. Perhaps we are entering a time of extroversion that witnesses the turning of *Geist* into an un-*geistige* world, better for people and only vaguely appreciative of another world's discovery that beauty and its indifference can make a life worth living.

SIX

Indifferent Freedom

> It was the large idea, though. . . . Which is perhaps
> necessarily formless, except in the traveler's mind.
> I mean that it can't be comprehensive, like a single
> objective, or done conclusively.
> —Shirley Hazzard, *The Great Fire*

Indifference" suggests detachment. Not necessarily total detachment, but detachment in relation to something. It might be the detachment maintained by keeping a certain distance, a certain space. Detachment can also happen as a space of perceiving or judging or the space of dispersion and disconnection, a spatial happening without attachment to what takes place in it. However else we characterize it, detachment indicates holding apart. As this chapter progresses I will say that narration can have a spatial aspect of detachment and that this aspect composes one kind of severe freedom. But before we reach this point I will make some further observations about detachment and tell you what a friend of mine says about what Plato says about the soul's detachments. Appearing and detachment have a remarkable connection according to that account, one that has been noticed for a long time in Western thought, and the connection is found in the very occurrence of specific things. We will find a certain attunement to the indifferent, appearing occurrence of things in narration, a severity that is not to be resolved but might be appreciated in its beauty and abruptness.

The philosopher David Hume, presented in two interpretations, will give us a modern view of what he calls the mind's native situation of indifference. Our predisposition to probabilities and flexibility will come to the fore, a certain amiability that counsels ethical caution (as distinct to "overheated" sentiments) and that offers freedom without anguish and accorded to the mind's indifferent liberty. We will then turn to narrative space, the freedom of variation, and finally the abrupt severity of indifferent freedom, sharply held apart from consolation and articulated remarkably in Robinson Jeffers's "Apology for Bad Dreams." Throughout this chapter that freedom peculiar to distance and indifference will hold sway and will pose the possibility of differentiating ourselves according to a degree of separation that holds us apart, not only from ourselves but also from whatever appears with us.

Holding apart can signify a measure of indifference: Socrates' Good (in the *Republic*), for example, in its self-enactment, holds apart from souls that seem to enjoy its overflow and that it seems to draw and ground. It is indifferent, in the sense of neutral and without interest, to the very souls for which it forms a strange measure. It does not seem to care for souls. It simply enacts itself and provides without interest an impartial measure of soullife even as it provides connection and order among the soul's beings. This indifference of self-enactment appears also in souls as they show themselves as open sites of appearing. Souls let shine forth, on this account, whatever is there to shine. As sites of appearing they compose a detached neutrality regarding the appearing of what appears (regardless of the interests of spirit or the purposes of wisdom), and this neutrality accompanies the soul's forceful, if conflicted, partialities and perspectives as well as its drive toward ordered identity.

We experience indifference of detachment when someone is without empathy and is not affected by our feelings and emotions—a detachment that we might find especially troubling in individuals whom we describe as morally insensitive or sociopathological. We also experience detached indifference when we are ignored—not hated or actively rejected, just ignored.

Indifferent detachment on a cosmic scale can be recognized by a sense of fate when an outcome appears destined regardless of people's effort and goodwill. Or when we, suffering, see things of great beauty that are utterly detached from our pain as well as from our identities and lives. It's strange, this connection of beauty and indifference, and I want to hold it in mind, although I have no idea what to do with it or about it in its stark refusal of my inclinations toward pragmatic relevance and an ethics of comparison.

Omar Rivera, about whom I will say more, in a series of informal discussions and notes, pointed out to me the connection of indifference and detachment at the very beginning of disciplined Western philosophy. Disruption is the key to Omar's insight, a series of disruptions found in Plato's dialogues that build on each other and help to form a very strange mosaic of indifferent connections. Such disruption carries a Pythagorean sensibility that runs through Plato's thought, a sensibility attuned to the importance for people of dimensions of reality that are indifferent to people. I imagine that such a sensibility not only trails off into prehistoric mythologems and rituals but also forms a forceful dimension of awareness in our reflective tradition. The force can be felt as negative when people react against it by contradiction and refusal—by believing, for example, that a grounding meaning of indifference is found in loving care or personal identity and intention. It can be positive when people cultivate recognitions of neutral carelessness in the lives of things and thereby affirm an important aspect of their world. Whether positive or negative, the force of a sense of indifference seems to produce theoretical and practical problems as people attempt to understand and live in their connections with each other and their environments. Such questions arise as the following: Does human caring have any significance beyond its own happening? What difference does ignoring or refusing the dimension of indifference make? In the face of vast indifference, should people sacrifice themselves? Learn not to care for themselves? Learn how not to care? Or care more intensely? Care for what or whom?

Omar thinks that the occurrence of disruptions in Plato's dialogues is a good place to begin to think about the importance of "indifference" in our lineage. Disruption takes place in the dialogues as Socrates makes multiple beginnings when he approaches an issue, for example, or when different aspects of the soul, such as spiritedness or appetitiveness, come to interruptive and conflictual expression in conversations and displace lines of focused thought. The disruptions show a region that is not under the jurisdiction of any of the interests and moods that take place within it, a space of disruption, we might say tentatively, that lacks rational order or even an economy of desire. Socrates also recognizes processes of dispersion in the soul itself due to its conflictual forces of appetite, spirit, and intellect. Not only do the appetites seek satisfactions without consideration of unified identity, for example, they also move the soul in multiple directions without interest in consistency or coherence: They themselves constitute drives toward dispersion. Spiritedness, on the other hand, is interested in unified identity and is at odds with the appetites. In its forceful difference from them it interrupts their way of being and seeks the dominance that an achievement of unity requires; but in *its* interruptive force it contributes in spite of its interest to the soul's disruption—it disrupts the appetites' dispersed pursuit of pleasures and carries out this disruption in continuing conflict with them. Its drive toward measured unity thus contributes to a dispersion in the soul, a drive that the appetites ignore or struggle against. A series of detachments between these soul-capacities, each moving away from the other, marks the soul's life as drives for pleasure hold themselves apart from a drive for unity, and spirit seeks measured detachment from the immediacy of appetitive forces. Spirit's intention is to be unmoved by them while the appetites resist its control in their search for satisfaction. The soul itself thus appears as a site of disruption and appears detached from the various interests that define its conflictual space. Omar says that the soul is always an indifferent site of appearing; that is, *conflicts* are *attunements* to its own indifferent occurrence.

Further, he notes, the soul in one of its aspects, as Plato describes it, experiences a desire to look, to find the intellect's pleasure of gazing: The soul in this perspective is inclined to detach itself from particularities enough to enjoy seeing what is to be seen. That intellectual inclination characterizes a predisposition to the neutrality of sight, to withdrawal from narrowing involvements for the sake of that distance necessary for simply gazing, no matter what a person sees. This curious indifference to what is manifest and the soul's indifferent capacity to allow manifestness forecast a kind of indifferent contemplation that the soul calls for (with interest). They also herald the idea that specific orders and identities accompany rather than overcome absence of unity and identity in the soul's occurrence. The intellect seems to be aligned in its pleasure of gazing with appetitive intentions in this sense: Both the intellect and the appetites are oriented to an important extent by what is outside of the soul and not by spirit's intention to consolidate soul's own force of identity. In their outward orientation, intellectual and appetitive intuitions tend toward the disruption of calculated, spirited self-realization. Intellectual activity moves away from spirited self-actualization to allow seeing what is there to be seen, and the appetites simply seek satisfactions among the offerings of the environment.

Even the soul's contemplation of the things of highest worth seems to invoke a withdrawal of highly specified identity and the boundaries of unified beings. Contemplation returns to the soul, considerably washed and brushed, when compared to curious attention, with profound detachment, not the detachment of dispersions but not that of singular self-actualized identities either: a different kind of detachment and indifference that we will look at more closely—look at it by detaching ourselves from the meaning of "identity" and "detachment"? We will have to see.

Omar points out that spiritedness is, for Plato, an ally of calculation. It is properly the power to find and follow measures, to find out how to achieve adherence among differences, and thus to find identities. It recognizes distinctions in their interconnections and searches out the measure appropriate to distinctions and their proportions in the unities they compose. Spiritedness is a serious-minded function of soul. It marks limits. It seeks steadiness of connections, security for values and their integrity, and clarity among distinctions. It establishes stances proper to different things. It is thoroughly interested, involved, and partial.

Omar observes, however, that spiritedness is also significantly limited by its kind of high-minded calculation. It is no friend of that depth of soul where stances and partialities begin to fade, where Eros and Hades dwell, and where noncalculative movements give measure and even high-mindedness another look. Spiritedness is even blind to its own depth, its own eventuating difference from stances and specific rules for forces, its own incalculable passions and shining. In its spiritedness the soul sees only the limits of formulations and ordered discourses. It does not see inarticulate depth that is more closely aligned with chaos and night than with mathematical order and metaphysical thought. (In a moment of spiritedness I asked Omar if he really thought this thought is in Plato and not primarily in a contemporary emphasis brought to Plato. Appropriately for the context Omar assured me this is a measured, correct, and proper reading of Plato's dialogue.) In order to reach the depth of both discourse and the soul's life, we need the space of interruptions and the dispersion of clear progression. We need an interruption and the dispersion that goes with it, interruption and dispersion that are indifferent to spirited intelligence—not the destruction of spirited accomplishment, mind you, but its interruption. We need that distancing afforded by interruption that removes us from a dominance of identity's value and from an accompanying emphasis on presence. This interruptive opening, Omar said, invokes detachment from the organic unity of a well-functioning identity. It—the interruptive opening—makes available to people not only the limits of the value of adherence but also a holding apart that is indigenous to such interruption—an indifference to identity that seems to accompany the achievement of identity. This indifference is not so much appetitive unconcern for measure and calculation. It is rather a holding apart characteristic of noncalculable dimensions of life, uncaring, neutral equivalence in the happening of shining, coming to appear, and passing away; it is manifest in the interruptive opening and allowance of connections, disjunctions, and dispersions. The interruptions in Platonic dialogues that Omar talked about open out to faceless dimensions, dimensions that do not have identity or intention. I would name (in a spirited moment) such dimensions the indifference of appearing and letting appear. Omar refined that name by pointing out that for Plato the soul is the site of appearing—not a particular "who" or a calculated "what," but a site whose eventuation is not ruled by the eidetic dimensions in appearing. The site of appearing introduces, he said, sheer foreignness vis-à-vis anything that is recognizable as something, and this site introduces inconstancy vis-à-vis any sustained event. Such introductions bring to bear the soul's perceptive depth that becomes accessible in indifferent detachments from discursive meaning and from spirited identity.

Embedded in Omar's observations is his recognition of a deep linkage between what Socrates says about the soul's several perspectives and the way Plato writes the dialogues. I use the adjective "deep" to connect with Omar's use of that word to describe the soul's noncalculative site of no identity that becomes available, especially because of detachments in the texture of the dialogues as well as in the soul's operation. This is an odd linkage in the sense that it is subject to more or less accurate description but also constitutes a deviant joining of eidetic and noneidetic factors. The dialogue's presentation of contradictory positions, virtual characters, and hypothetical situations in its linkage to the soul composes a dialogical expression of detachment from singular and present identity, detachment that comprises the soul's and the dialogue's depth as both soul and dialogue stretch to dimensions of life that will not be named properly or recognized as anything: indifference to identity reached sometimes by detachment, by what Omar called "foreignness-in-appearing." In his terms this linkage cannot be forged adequately by spirit, and it can be known only in attunement to the dimension of reality that is without concern—that of indifference. With attention to this dimension we come to see intellectually that the very account of the soul's differentiation and identity is insufficient to the soul's reach, that a disruption of the account can be as much an activity of soul as the account is in its most sensitive, eidetic discipline. Such attention to the dimension of indifference makes a considerable difference as the soul reflects itself in Plato's writing. And with this thought we can see why Omar finds so important the detachments and interruptions that occur in the dialogues: They reflect what of the soul is always foreign to its *self*, what we know only in detachment from eidetic identity and unity.[1]

Plato's dialogues reflect also his detachment as he writes, creates images, and gives written life to characters and thoughts. That is a detachment all the more pronounced in Plato's indebtedness to Phoenician culture for the medium of his presentation—indebtedness, in fact, to untellable influences and events that comprise not only his medium of expression but also his language and perceptiveness. As he perceived and wrote, I speculate, different foreign cultures, histories, and forces continuously detached him from the Greek rootage of which he was most aware—a strange and unsettling melding and detaching happening at once that probably made some part of his awareness inchoately uneasy with writing and with some of the ways he perceived and presented events around him.

In addition to indifference's and detachment's apparentness in the occurrence of appearing, they are also apparent in the play of influences and

---

1. Omar made interesting observations about justice, which he described as constituting the soul's depth and as indifferent in the sense of impartial. He distinguished, in a spirited way, the power of justice to determine the soul's "ownness" and the appearing of justice. A unifying neutrality characterizes the power of justice but detached indifference vis-à-vis the power of justice characterized the appearing of this power. The distinction between power and the appearing of power is significant in this discussion of indifference. The distinction suggests, in the case of justice, that lack of interest and discrimination accompany a strong interest in justice.

events that figure in any articulate expression. Indifference was not a specific problem for Plato, I believe. Mythological formulations such as Night and Chaos and Gaia, Light (the very element of Zeus's divinity), Plato's own sense for form, the mystical power of number, the neutrality of *phusis* and fate—a sense of indifference pervaded classical Greek formulations and awareness. There was no news in the indifference of occurrence, and were there in that culture what we now think of as a sense of history, I hypothesize that Plato would not have been surprised by the indifference of lineages' enactments and of plays of influence. There were other problems to worry about like the soul and justice as well as change, permanence, and, in Plato's case, cultivation of alertness proper to unwritable and usually hidden dimensions of what is real—dimensions, appropriate attention to which can make a huge difference for thought and to all the other important capacities of soul. But a certain neutrality and holding apart from identity and human sensibility? That wasn't a problem. Such detachment comes with the appearing of whatever appears. It describes not just the way the world is. It describes the possibility of any coherence and life.

As Plato helped to give birth to Western philosophy, he invested the detachment of artistic expression in the inception. He expressed his thought by means of dialogical narratives, giving reflective life to an ensemble of characters and conflicts and reflecting at once his mind's life in a work quite separate from him, distant enough to allow its own perceptions and considerations, something that reflected his own experience of soul as well as of a persona he loved. His dialogues compose forceful reflections, the force of mirroring, a force that detaches as it connects and that destabilizes as it establishes presence. That persona, Socrates, in its loving and reflective force, allowed Plato to see himself in a remarkable light—in a distance, indeed, in a detachment of reflection and love, erotic and intelligent in its mirroring power and in its destabilization of any sense of fixed identity that Plato might have had. Mirroring, I repeat, destabilizes. Lovers and artists may not enjoy secure senses of stable identity as they mirror themselves in the beloved or in the work or art. Like actors, they know that identities have their hour and are subject to forces beyond their control as they mutate and transform—watery reflections in the mirroring events—especially as they are taken from themselves by forces other to themselves or when they are dislodged in their identities as they step back from themselves and allow another to move them as though the other were their selves—allow another to identify their selves. The lover is forever stepping back of (in this case) his own claims and manner of life, filled as he is by the presence of the beloved, lost to himself with the beloved's life; and the artist knows the inconstancy of muses, moods, intuitive processes, and formations of insight as well as the strange loss of self in the self's artistic presentation. They all are at the mercy of movements they do not control and that destabilize their sense of who, exactly, they are. The lover undergoes such destabilization as he, in the presence of the beloved who mirrors him back to himself, detaches himself from the power of his self-interest, steps back, in his love, of singular self-direction and fixes his attention on his beloved, losing even the right of possession. He finds himself anew, in some ways broken if also reborn in reflection: an unsettled and destabilized reflective distance, filled with connection, passion, and interest, suffused with an indifference of happening, as though nothing cared with all this caring, as though gods were laughing.

I expect that an artist like Plato finds destabilization in the process of detaching himself from a measure of control over his characters and the directions their talk takes. They move him as he conceives them. The depth (to use Omar's sense of the word), a region beyond eidetic control, of Plato's work happens in part where continuity is broken, arguments fail, and an odd sense of both lack of completion and insight join—a dialogical depth where something more than the sum total of meanings and signs seems to emerge and to defy direct communication. I imagine that Plato the writer experienced the detachment that can come with such events, not unlike the detachment that can come with the arrival of something beautiful. You can't do much about something beautiful (clutch a sunrise?), although in the detached and fetching distance of what is beautiful you can do whatever you like in its presence. Plato, I imagine, found in such events of communicative depth as they happened in his dialogues the satisfactions of a creative facilitator when he steps back of what he has helped to bring about, and sees it, knows it, shining before him with the indifferent distance of detached reflection.

So many dimensions: preoccupied if not obsessed assertiveness on the part of the artist, measured *lack* of control, as well as detached control—a discipline of not holding too tightly, of allowing the unexpected to happen—in conceptual and expressive activity. The silent operation of elements constitutive of perceptiveness and the media of expression, the independence of the work of art that owes at least its artifactual existence to an author, a detachment in the work from the work by the life that the work addresses, at best an accomplishment that measures its own success in terms of incompletion and broken authority. Not to mention the odd indifference of the written signs, the experiential explicitness and intensity that their abstract functions can occasion, the indifference of temporal passage and translation, the indifference of appearing. And the indifference and detachment of the eventuation of the work with all these dimensions—its being there apparently as whatever it is.

Plato's philosophical work as an artist who loved Socrates, work with so many dimensions of attachment and detachment, stabilization and destabilization, differentiation and indifference—this artistic work that helped to engender Western philosophy carries with it a dimension of awareness interwoven into which is the affective issue of being a singular event with interests and passions living in a disinterested and impassive world. A dimension of indifference accompanies our most intense experiences of differentiation (as well as our milder ones). Omar speaks of the depth of soul in its irreducibility to any overarching unity when he speaks of this indifference. The stakes for him, I believe, are those associated with intense experiences of being alive as distinct from superficiality and shallow character. The stakes, in other words, have to do with beauty and ugliness incorporated in the fabric of individual lives because the content and quality of lives appear to depend in part on people's appropriation of this dimension, whether by covering it over, denying it, or accepting it. One implication in Plato's work is that the positive appropriation of differentiation with indifference can be expressed, and perhaps best expressed, when people live their lives as works of art, looking to weave with a certain detachment the changing, given elements into an event that holds relatively steady in its displacing, destabilizing incompletion. This weaving from a changing, given, multiply interrupted position can reflect itself only with an immediacy of detachment, not simply detachment from "self," but detachment also in the event that the weaving process is—weaving detachment into the work of being this self-reflective event, mirroring it as it takes place.

"An immediacy of detachment." "Immediacy" suggests presence. "Detachment" suggests a withdrawal of presence, disengagement, distance, and indifference (as in "a detached point of view"). When people are detached they assume an emphasized singularity. They lack a measure of empathic connection. They distance themselves in relation to something. To carry out their techniques and to present what they have in mind, for example, artists, like surgeons, need distance vis-à-vis their work—not only the distance for critical judgment but also the more radical distance that allows disciplined expression, an immediate distance, a lived and concentrated distance that displaces whatever of the artist is irrelevant to the work, a distance that might allow something new to happen. Detached from major parts of their lives, detached from the paint or words or motions so that they (the paint, etc.) might come into their own, invested in the work at a distance to it and themselves, artists can function in an immediacy of detachment that feels odd in a context of habitual regularity and recognition. Detachment in its immediacy intensifies nonhabitual singularity. It sets things apart. But it also sets persons off from themselves, brings with it psychological hiatus, borders of persona with extended distances among them, a loosened fabric of identity—it brings with it people who are more indifferent than usual, more uncaring about more things, disinterested in normally interesting events. More forgetful. More preoccupied and distracted. Now and then more "creative." More facilitative of what is new and foreign.

ANOTHER KIND OF INDIFFERENCE:
CARELESS PHILOSOPHY

I turn now to Catherine Kemp's and Annette Baier's work on Hume, especially on what Hume called the mind's "native situation of indifference" and what Baier calls careless philosophy.[2] A kind of careless indifference might well describe aspects of artistic endeavor, but does it describe parts of the life of modern theoretical work and understanding? An implication in Plato's work is that people properly make their lives into works of art, and we found that artistic work can intensify worldly carelessness. Do people in the modern period in their perceptive, intelligent experience also discover in that experience dimensions of indifference and carelessness? Is indifference immediately invested in modern theoretical activity?

Catherine Kemp finds her access to mental indifference by means of Hume's consideration of acts of mind as distinct to its passive states. She reads the *Treatise* as showing what the mind does with its impressions: "The mind's indifference and its determination in experience" is her apt phrasing as she brings attention to the mind's active relation with its objects. Determinations happen by virtue of the contents of perceptions: Perceived objects are specific things such as hard surfaces, soft pillows, cold ice, and warm coffee. Contents have forces—the ice on hot skin, for example—that enjoy varying degrees of liveliness and that provide distinct impressions of distinct things in mental activity. But it's in mental activity that indifference resides, specifically in "mere conception."

For Hume, mere conceptions are ideas as such, "faint and languid" mental formations. "The act-aspect of ideas are at least initially non-lively or

---

2. This conversation will be within the limits of Professor Kemp's article "Experience Matters: Indifference and Determination in Hume's *Treatise*," *Journal of Speculative Philosophy* 16, no. 4 (2002), and Professor Baier's chapter, "Philosophy in This Careless Manner," in *A Progress of Sentiments: Reflections on Hume's Treatise* (Cambridge, Mass.: Harvard University Press, 1991). References will appear in the text in parentheses referencing each author's text in the respective discussions. I am indebted to Professor Kemp, in addition to her article, for several conversations on the topic of this section and for directing me to Professor Baier's book.

mere conceptions" (245). The "mere" aspect of conceptions means that the mind has not connected a mental object with existence—has not, for example, found the object, ice cube, coldly alive on warm skin. A mere conception is without belief or sensuous experience regarding the existence of its object. A mere conception is thus indeterminate, unsupported by the regularity of frequent repetitions or associations: The mind simply "entertains the idea (as content) of an object without believing in the existence of the object, a feature of the mind Hume calls 'indifference'" (247). The mind is neutral in the sense that it can look without partisanship at many sides and aspects of ideas: "the contrary of every matter of fact is still possible" (quoted at 247). The indifferent aspect of mental acts, their impartiality, describes their "looseness," not a global, quasi-ontological anterior mental state of absolute neutrality, but the uncommitted quality of ideas that are not collected and joined by beliefs based on experienced, past repetitions, custom, or regular orders of contiguity and succession (246). We may think of this kind of indifference as neutral liberty in which people may anticipate alternatives and experience simultaneously with determinations a measure of freedom for correction and innovation. While such indifference is not "global," Hume does call it "native" and suggests a dimension of mental activity that is not eradicated by determinations in experience. The chancy aspect of experienced connections finds, I assume, a resonance in the mind's native situation of indifference: Indifference figures option, absence of ontological necessity, availability of transformations, and the possibility of redetermination (247, 254, footnotes 20 and 21).

Kemp thus shows that in Hume's account of acts of conception indifference figures a looseness, a lack of determined compulsion as well as a situation that is available for mental redetermination. The human mind has impartiality that happens as the "shape" of ideas happens. Or, stated another way, probability and lack of determination indwell conceptual, shaping activity: Determination and indifference happen together. Experience will lead us to believe, for example, that where there has been a certain continuity of events—the sun's rising after night—we may expect that continuity to continue. But the mind is attuned to an absence of iron-clad necessity and is natively open to options: Its indifference sets the mind apart from its own beliefs, not eliminating them or their importance but reserving in its nondetermination an often faint sense of "it might not have to be this way," a relatively quiet sense, not one of disbelief, but of impartial nonbelief. Ideas in their activity compose, it seems, an inchoate and not-very-lively awareness that no set of determinations necessarily has the final word for the future or for any mental connection. I agree with Kemp's observation that this account is not properly described as skepticism. It is rather an account of indifference in conception and experience that addresses a coherence of determination and a lack of determination in mental activity. It is not a claim that there is no true knowledge. It is an account of the way true knowledge takes place.

The mind's predisposition to probabilities rather than only to the constancy suggested by lively beliefs and habits means that it is attuned to the dimension of chance that seems invested in experienced connections and contiguities. "In mere conception, the mind is indifferent to its confirmation or disconfirmation. In a probability of causes, none of the 'sides' . . . prevails. In a probability of causes, for either 'side' to prevail, it must exceed the other 'side' in the number of instances in which it appears" (259). The mind's indifferent predisposition thus composes neutrality before competing beliefs, beliefs that are lively, forceful, mental acts. Nondetermination with determinations, neutrality with partisanship, disinterest with interest: The mind as Hume finds it is strangely differentiated with indifference and is imaginatively able because of its native, largely concealed impartiality. The mind comprises an active space of indifference whereby it can play with alternatives, construct strange figures of mental aspects, simply gaze at other constructions, delineate among forceful options, and act in other subjunctive manners with matters of factual and customary determinations. The mind, as Hume finds it, is prepared—in principle, always prepared—to reevaluate the contents of conceptions according to new experiences.

In this account the mind's temporal and flexible life is due to indifference in its enactments. This indifference means that each act of conception with its contents is subject to redetermination: The indeterminate loose quality of mere conception means that redetermination is not only possible but highly likely and that mental activity happens with a dynamism otherwise unavailable to activity controlled by custom. The mind is a dynamic state of awareness due to its continuous availability for variations in experience. "Indifferently" is an appropriate adverb for the mind's continuing and varying determination and redetermination in experience, according to Kemp (251).

Kemp also notes, as a consequence of Hume's account of the mind's native situation of indifference, a basic "amenability" of relations that impact the liberty of imagination: Binding relations in mental acts are amenable with each other in their simultaneous and imaginative, that is, indifferent, character (252). The insistent and forceful quality of vivid experiences and binding customs is qualified by mental indifference, and in this qualification different directions and forces gain an ability for constructive, mentational connection. The mind's indifference gives regions of undecidability—spaces of neutrality, as it were—that permit change and transformation.

Attuned as indifference is to the chancy aspect of experiences, "amenability" thus suggests caution as people think in the force of habits and custom, suggests an attitude less inclined to assertion than to question and experiment, suggests quietly that assertive certainty can comprise a lost touch with the amenable ways experience and thinking happen in the context of the mind's native situation. The emphasis that Hume places on experience and experiment for disciplined thought thus joins his distaste for metaphysical speculation. It joins also his recognition that the temporality and liberty of mental acts intimate that fitting ways of thinking will be attuned to their own element of indifference. This intimation suggests a shift in feeling (or, in Hume's terminology, sentiment) from an anxious and heavy insistence on certainty to a less weighty predisposition, to a lightness of mind that many lively impressions and customs do not allow in their singular stances. This is a felt inclination toward experimentation, perhaps an affirmation of reciprocity among experiences that allows dominance to the meaning of none.

Such a fit of indifference and attitudes thus could be found in a chastened intellect, one that attempts passionately to hold in check those forces in experience that declare themselves with insistence on their authoritative repetition. Such forces have mental energy and appear in expressions of habit-formed dispositions and prevailing, affective tendencies and moods. Affective patterns—orders of feeling—arise with beliefs and habits. They can fuel inclinations, for example, toward solitary activity or convivial pleasure, toward certain kinds of identity and practice. When the affections are obsessive in their habitual patterns, mental events will intensify in their insistence and repetition and produce rigidity of order as well as types of unhappiness.

Obsessive differentiations often express a disposition to hold one fast, to resist change and inconsistency, to resist even the very processes of affective life; and Hume, according to Baier, had to learn how to appropriate his affectional life, to release himself from an obsessive concern for consistency and harmony. He had to learn how to live reflectively with inconstancy and inconsistency of his feelings, before he could think with the full life of mind: "it is not intellect but 'my mind all collected with itself' . . . which takes up 'those subjects about which I have not so many disputes in the course of my reading and conversation'" (22). A "mind all collected with itself" means in this context an active and affirming engagement with the multiple and often contradictory figurations that compose an identity. The phrase suggests self-awareness that prioritizes differences in an identity rather than the seeming monotonal constancy of one kind of function (refined logical reflections, for example) or characteristic (e.g., solitary introversion). Relief from reflective obsession as well as from an "uneasiness" that comes with it allowed Hume a measure of creativity and lightness of mind, in addition to a broadened scope of recognition and satisfaction that Baier finds exemplary for philosophers (22).

An obsessive mind might begin to change when a person finds himself willing and able to recognize the illusions that play major roles in his life and the protection of which defines part of the obsession's function.[3] Baier emphasizes Hume's urge to expose illusion and contradiction—the very urge that fired his excesses in theorizing—as important in his discovery that his theoretical absorption was based in part on illusions of solitary independence in his thought and of the possibility that rational existence could be without self-contradiction (18). He also found that his own rational life was based on the illusion that false consciousness could be eliminated. In fact, he found that a rational life is so invested in customs and beliefs with their illusions and unfounded assumptions that a reasonable person must see that neither absolute certainty nor uncontestable goodness are possible, much less an identity founded on harmonious constituents. There is a degree of neutrality along with serious commitments and identity traits in a reasonable life due to oppositional and contradictory aspects basic to a person's experience and consciousness.

A "brain" "overheated" by the custom-oriented and single-minded suasion of a given body of beliefs will overlook its own custom-oriented and experiential composition and, in the name of consistency and rightness, will become a major contradiction for itself: It will irrationally stabilize itself by authoritative illusions and accomplish the opposite of its aim of being rationally consistent with itself (19–20). In the language I have been using, a person so accentuates a specific differentiation that he ignores the indifference that comes with it and compromises its authority to control a broad segment of experience. In effect, Hume discovered that the complexity and incoherence of human experience compose a dimension of unconcern and carelessness—of indifference—as distinct to rational interest in simple and straightforward correctness. To be rational on his terms came to mean recognition of philosophy as based in dispositions and directed in significant measure by sentiments that are self-supporting and not based in

---

3. These remarks do not address severe obsession but rather persistent preoccupations that are more like a habit of mind than a debilitating neurosis or psychosis. The excessive quality of a habitual obsession is in connection with diminished or ignored aspects of a person's life. I might, for example, be obsessed with theoretical rigor to such a degree that I do not notice that my friend is feeling sad, or I might habitually overlook many of my own feelings in my obsession with completing tasks. Baier emphasizes Hume's early lack of explicit awareness of his feelings and this kind of liveliness. This discussion does not address problems that arise when people deal with obsessions obsessively.

a "higher" intentionality. His recognition of the complexity and incoherence of mental life meant that refined thinking became more a matter of satisfying a certain disposition than one of bringing something ultimate or ontologically fundamental to expression. The kind of seriousness that accompanies many philosophical pursuits is a symptom of overheated determinations that have lost touch with the indifference that turns their boundaries to nothing at all.

Baier finds Hume's movement through and away from reflective obsession and to "mild and moderate sentiments" to allow him enough "mental stability" and breadth of reference for critical self-consciousness and clarity in his efforts to understand people's experiences and practices (23–24). This is a movement toward what she calls "a broader discipline of reflection on human nature" than is usually allowed in our philosophical tradition (25). "A cautious observation of human life," she says, an "inexact human science of self-conscious human nature," is an undertaking that is "careless" in the sense that it is "free of tyrannizing obsessions, including an over-dedication to the new philosophy itself." This way of thinking "may be done more by an instructive series of mutually contradicting, self-correcting theses than by a polished but static consistent system" (26). This is a kind of moderation and tolerance for contradiction that arises when people do not attempt to force the authority of a set of determinations on the whole of experience and meaning and learn to live with the mind's native, indifferent liberty.

IMPARTIAL PRESENTATIONS

Nonjudgmental presentations of different and often conflicting situations require operative neutrality on the part of the speaker or writer. When an author presents criminal or unjust situations without a hero who shows us what is right and good or without correction of the injustice or even without apparent judgment—when we encounter such impartial presentations we might well pass our own judgments on both the presented situation and the author. Indifferent presentations of what we consider very bad people and situations are usually offensive. Although I am not looking for moral lessons when I see a movie or visit a museum, I do want confirmation of something I recognize as good, such as a basic value or success in the defense of something I affirm (a struggling family, a gay couple who love each other, disgust over futile wars, a positive symbol, an experience of beauty). If all I find is bleak "realism," why bother? No joy, tears, loathing, anger, elevation of spirit, release from boredom, agony of commitments under stress or magnificence? Act without such experiences? I can't imagine it. But there is another dimension that also seems important: a detached neutrality accompanying the value-laden determinations, a space of telling that allows whatever may be told, a space of presentation and appearing, of differentiation, amenability, unreconciled conflict, entertainment of options, probabilities, accident, connection and departure, a space of variation without intention. One aspect of this nonjudgmental dimension shows a prospect simply for telling, for presenting multiple points of view, the kind of freedom that allows presentations not ordered by authoritative, moral opinion.

In the absence of judgmental order we do not find overarching hierarchies of value to accompany differentiating hierarchies in the work. Even though we find perspective and selection, we do not find a likelihood of reparations for offenses or atrocities, rewards for virtue, or satisfactions for injuries. Such expiations might or might not occur; there is no order in this dimension of occurrence and mentation that requires them. What happens when events are presented in writing that attempts coordination with its own nonjudgmental space as well as with the wild and accidental quality of ordinary events?

In *Atonement*,[4] Ian McEwan tells a story, a direct and simple one in its primary outline, that is complicated by chance events, multiple perspectives, and misperceptions. McEwan connives with these perversions of good order in their telling. The part of him that is in charge of telling the story of an almost tragic love appears as a seventy-seven-year-old woman who, perhaps, is telling her own story and that of her sister before she, the narrator, fades in an oblivion of dementia. Connivent, chance occurrences conjure the details of a family of lives under the command of the told character of the narrator (who is a member of that family). The determined order of the story and its grammatical medium—and especially the order of the teller's good intentions—make vivid senseless accidents, differences of perception, coincidences, and spontaneity vivid in the reality of fictional events. Deterioration and impending oblivion echo no order throughout the story's sensible structure as it unwinds past events in a space without determined presence.

Here is the story in bare outline:

In 1935 thirteen-year-old and prodigious Briony writes a play, "The Trials of Arabella." It is a melodrama with a poetic prologue about a "spontaneous" young heroine who willfully and naively runs off with an irre-

---

4. Ian McEwan, *Atonement* (New York: Doubleday, 2001). References will appear in the text in parentheses.

sponsible foreign count. Its message: "love which did not build on a foundation of good sense was doomed" (3). The story is drenched with poetic justice as life's lessons unfold for poor Arabella until good judgment returns to her and she finds happiness with a "medical prince" (4). Such justice and the reign of good sense, however, rule only in Briony's play. From the time she writes her play and the narrator tells the story of its writing with affectionate, ironic humor, nothing happens justly, and good sense has only moments of limited influence.

Briony, who requires a tidy world, misperceives an unconventional incident at a fountain involving her sister, Cecilia, and Robbie, an accidental incident that begins their intemperate, passionate love for each other and leads to a series of completely unexpected events that make impossible her play's planned performance that evening. Attracted by an odd noise several hours after the incident in the fountain, she walks into a darkened study where, in yet another event that has no place in her immature and conventional world, her sister and Robbie are wildly engaged in intercourse while standing in a shadowed corner, a happenstance that she interprets as one of awful physical abuse wrecked on Cecilia. This and her first misperception are compounded by her reading a letter Robbie sent, with Briony as carrier, to Cecilia in which, against all odds, he declares his love for her. Unfortunately, he sent by mistake an earlier, vividly erotic, and, in the social context, obscene version.

A house visitor, the fifteen-year-old Lola, who intimidates even Briony and of whom Briony is jealous, is the object of Paul's (another adult guest) sexual advances. In a late-night search of the grounds for two rascally twins who have "run away" primarily to get attention, Briony finds Lola by a lake in a sexual situation with a shadowy figure (Paul), who quickly steps out of her view in the darkness. Lola, ever deceptive and manipulative, behaves hysterically and confirms Briony's hasty conjecture that it was Robbie forcing himself on her, a conjecture that quickly becomes a certainty. Robbie, a most sympathetic and innocent character, is wrongly charged and convicted of raping a minor on the basis of Briony's and Lola's testimony. Cecilia's and his love survives the terrible crisis, although she breaks totally from her family, and he, to get an early release from prison, joins the British army, serves with distinction in France, and is wounded and becomes seriously ill during the gruesome retreat to Bray Dunes and Dunkirk.

As Briony matures she realizes what she has done. (Lola and Paul, both banal and insensitive people, later marry and maintain a silence, protected because of his wealth and power.) Briony becomes a nurse during the war under the strenuous, sacrificial conditions characteristic of such work in Britain at that time. In spite of Cecilia's and Robbie's cold hatred, she summons enough courage to confess her crime to them, her family, and the civil authorities. She comes through the accompanying abasement and emotional rejection with her self-esteem and artistic ability intact.

Cecilia's and Robbie's lives have been irreparably damaged, but they love each other with a rare intensity and can anticipate, at last, a life together in spite of the considerably reduced circumstances.

Not exactly Briony's tale of the spontaneous Arabella, but not entirely unlike it either. Let's turn to the telling of the story.

The gentle, sometimes mocking irony in the story's presentation of the young Briony is that of the storyteller, who is Briony in her seventies—the orderly, early adolescent, who wished for "a harmonious and organized world," wished for it so fervently, in fact, that she could not imagine herself as an agent of chaotic wrongdoing. This Briony who wrote to establish good order (with a sensible amount of suffering to correct mistakes and flaws of character) did not want to know of life's atrocities and horrors. She wanted "miniaturization. A world could be made in five pages" (7). Briony, the adult storyteller, presents her youthful self relentlessly but with light humor—not with forgiveness or condemnation and not quite with compassion. Rather, she presents herself as she presents all events in the story, with implacable exactness in the details of flaws, mistakes, ill will, and weakness as well as in the details of honesty, sickness, strength, ability, and affection. So many differences converge, often in conflict, sometimes finding a measure of positive resonance, generosity, and satisfaction, often diverging like ricocheting projectiles that literally or figuratively maimed people and left them crippled or dead. Her account of the retreating British army, partially ordered, partially in terrible chaos, often strafed and bombed by Stukas, both bereft and heroically served on the exposed beach of Bray Dunes—her accounts of the retreating army and the hospital that received the wounded speak not only of war's horror but also of the horror that can happen less dramatically and less observed in everyday life. And yet Briony's tone remains undisturbed. She looks for the details of war, sickness, friendship, love, courage, survival skills—the details of experience in extreme events—in order to see more clearly the range and reverberations in ordinary lives consequent to naiveté, banality, weakness, imperception, overwhelming circumstances, and selfishness—as well as those of imperfect kindness, firmness of mind, and, above all, love. She combs archives, memoirs, and letters, looking, I suppose, in part to present by intensified reflection on a grander scale what she has done and its consequences, as well as to present resonances in storytelling and the availability of what may be told.

She condemns no one. She justifies no one. She tells as severely as she can the story with its many enlivening "unscored dissonances" and terrible events (271). No sacrifice could make reparation for the injustices and suffering (although an effort in that direction by a character should be noticed). No good deed could make amends for the many destructions . . . unless atonement could be found in telling the story.[5]

Briony discovered early in her life that by telling a story you could have a world, possess it by writing it down. That was nothing like witnessing events that were outside of her range of understanding and control (35). That view of writing, however, mostly died under the impact of experience. Instead of minimalization and control, she opted for the liberty of presenting multiple perspectives and qualities of experience in shared events. There is a measure of authorial control, certainly, but it is inhibited, perhaps censored by the indifferent space of differences that is told in the telling of the various, often incompatible perspectives. No perspective rules, and the storyteller herself gives no hierarchical order to them.

Briony learned with excitement that she could write a scene from many points of view—with excitement because of "the prospect of freedom of being delivered from the cumbersome struggle between good and bad, heroes and villains. None of these [perspectives] was bad, nor were they particularly good. She need not judge. There did not have to be a moral. She need only show separate minds, as alive as her own, struggling with the idea that other minds were equally alive. . . . And only in a story could you enter these different minds and show how they had equal value. That was the only moral a story need have" (38). The now well-noted writer writes concerning herself: "Her fiction was known for its amorality, and like all authors . . . she felt obliged to produce a story line, a plot of her development that contained the moment when she became recognizably herself" (38).

The moment of self-recognition comes, Briony says, with memory, when memory is all that is left of an event. The gap between palpable events and memory of them—the gap that makes articulate perspective possible—is like that between individual experiences. Truth becomes "as

---

5. The love story ends when Briony finds Cecilia and Robbie, faces their unforgiving rage, tells them that Lola was with Paul that night by the lake in 1935, gives them additional information, and promises again (she had written to Cecilia) to inform under oath the authorities of the facts, retracting her earlier testimony and confessing her guilt. In addition, she will send "a long letter" to them, detailing everything relevant to her false testimony. No atonement is available—the full deed and its consequences were "fixed in the unchangeable past" (329). The only thing that counts is setting the record straight, objectively relieving Robbie of legal guilt, and presenting herself in a narrative as perpetrator of an injustice that will never be forgiven. But after the letters were written, "she knew what was required of her. Not simply a letter, but a new draft, an atonement, and she was ready to begin." Briony wrote those words in 1999, when she was seventy-seven. Finally that draft was completed. Although it should have been her first novel, it became her last. But McEwan's book is not finished with Briony's completion of the draft of her story, and the expected atonement is unavailable.

ghostly as invention" in the oblivion of past and unreachable presence (39). Robbie and Cecilia stood there, at the fountain in 1935, Cecilia soaking wet. When they left, a wet patch on the ground was all that remained. And a while later, Briony saw, nothing remained but the fountain surrounded by dry ground. Briony had to remember, to recall what happened. Not entirely *what* happened, but her perception of what happened, her no doubt inventive memory of a perception that itself was inventive with the force of limited experience and a very active imagination. The truth of what happened then was like the way truth in her stories happened. Not untrue, but slippery with its perspectival cast and distance of occurrence. And the spatial environment of that memory—the space of the happening at the fountain with its fateful immediacy, that of their absence with a wet spot remaining, that of dried ground and no trace of the fateful, complex, palpable happening—and the environment of Briony's memory, the space of its variations and associations: those spaces resonant with indifference, a space of time's passage with richly textured, thoroughly specific events.

Further, Briony discovers herself once she has found enough distance to present herself and her disastrous crime with irony, humor, and mockery. That distance did not emerge for many years, and when it did it allowed what she describes as her amoral presentation to take shape and to achieve resonance with the neutral space of telling a story.

The place for telling emerges clearly in this writing: not a good space or a bad space. Not a moral one. But a space for moralities and truths and much else. That span can be told by impartial presentations of unranked, multiple perspectives in a partially shared, now remembered event. And in it Briony was able to present herself recognizably to herself, an accomplishment, I assume, that was impossible as long as she seriously looked for sensible reasons, moral understanding, or forgiveness. The neutrality of ironic humor was the ticket for this self-understanding.

The story's short remainder begins when Briony has completed the story of her, Lola's, and Paul's crime and of the lives of Cecilia and Robbie (as well as her included account of "the collective insanity of war") (333). She has just discovered that she has vascular dementia and can expect a process of small strokes, continuing loss of memory, and increased enfeeblement leading to total dependence before her death. She will not be able to publish her manuscript until after her death or those of Lola and Paul (now Lord and Lady Marshal) because of the prolonged and expensive litigation it would occasion. "The Marshals have been active about the courts since the late forties, defending their good names with a most expensive ferocity . . . one might almost think they have something to hide" (349). She goes to her seventy-seventh birthday party at the old manor house, now a hotel, where her youthful tale of spontaneous Arabella is played for the first time (its manuscript was found by one of her cousins who had a role in its failure to be produced sixty-four years earlier). The penultimate line of the melodrama is "Here's the beginning of love at the end of our travail." (The last line: "So farewell, kind friends, as into the sunset we sail" [348].)

In her last novel, in 1999, she leaves Cecilia and Robbie holding hands on the street as Nurse Briony, after their encounter, walks into the Waterloo subway station to buy her ticket to the hospital on the other side of London. The beginning of a life together in their remarkable love? Quite possibly. Although Briony reports that this was the last of several versions that she wrote—the telling space allows that kind of revision—the earlier drafts

> were pitiless. But now I can no longer think what purpose would be served if, say, I tried to persuade my reader, by direct or indirect means, that Robbie Turner died of septicemia at Bray Dunes on June 1940, or that Cecilia was killed in September of the same year by the bomb that destroyed Balham Underground station. That I never saw them that year. . . . How could that constitute an ending? What sense or hope or satisfaction could a reader draw from such an account? Who would want to believe that they never met again, never fulfilled their love? Who would want to believe that, except in the service of the bleakest realism? I couldn't do it to them. I'm too old, too frightened, too much in love with the shred of life that I have remaining. I face an incoming tide of forgetting and then oblivion. I no longer possess the courage of my pessimism. When I am dead . . . and the novel is finally published, we will only exist as my inventions. (350)

Her confession continues: "Briony will be as much of a fantasy as the lovers who shared a bed in Balham and enraged their landlady. No one will care what events and which individuals were misrepresented to make a novel. I know there's always a certain kind of reader who will be compelled to ask, But what *really* happened? The answer is simple: the lovers survive and flourish. As long as there is a single copy, a solitary transcript of my final draft, then my spontaneous, fortuitous sister and her medical prince survive to love" (352).

On the one hand, Briony wanted to tell the story of her, Lola's, and Paul's crime with no disguise or indirection: "the names, the places, the exact circumstances—I put it all there as a matter of historical record." And she follows Robbie's odyssey to Dunkirk by way of Bray Dunes with an equal attention to exactness of detail and direct engagement with historical atrocity. Briony wants concrete, accurate realism. On the other hand, Briony is a fictional character, a medium of distance for McEwan, a figure in a story whose truth is found in the telling. All characters, says the publisher's notice, "are the product of the author's imagination or are used fictitiously." Presumably that statement is not a fiction. But in the indifferent space of the novel Briony is alive, if terminally ill, carrying the enormous responsibility of writing about her own search for atonement and finding in the writing no possibility for it. She finds an indifference that comes with the difference of a story, giving her "no one, no entity or higher form that she can appeal to or be reconciled with, or that can forgive her. . . . The attempt was all" (350–51).

"All" is a lot. In the indifferent freedom of the novel, Briony opts, without necessity, for "a final act of kindness, a stand against oblivion and despair, to let my lovers live and to unite them at the end" (357). Would they ever forgive Briony? Briony's novel wasn't yet published. She still had memory and energy. Might they yet come to Briony's birthday party? There's still space and time. McEwan gave her that. Before he closed the final draft and let Doubleday publish it. Still, in the novel there's an "ever" quality. It could have happened, it always could have happened otherwise.

FREEDOM IN EXPERIENCE

I have used "space" when I referred to the dimension of indifference—the space of detachment and disruptions, for example, that of differences without superordinate identity, of ungrounded conflicts, mental liberty, amenability. This dimension of occurrences lacks definitive order, grounding stability, and any semblance of subjectivity. It is like a space of coincidences, spontaneities, connections with passing and perhaps contrary necessities. It occurs as a nondifferentiated dimension of differences. *A* nondifferentiated dimension of differences? *The* dimension of indifference? Yes. Difference from specific differentiations. Oddly without singularity, identity, or meaning in its happening, a region of experience that opens experience out of itself to nothing in particular, as though it were non-space, nothing, not even other. A dimension because in manifest occurrences it "is" merely without differentiation. Simple else than in experiences of determinate things.

I have located senses of this dimension in Omar Rivera's story of Plato's imagery of the soul, in Kemp's and Baier's interpretations of Hume's account of mind, and in McEwan's story of Briony's story, *Atonement*. In each case there has been a narrated narrator: Omar Rivera, Catherine Kemp, Annette Baier, Briony-McEwan. They compose telling differences that I tell about, localized interpreters and correspondents who allow conversations to arise and evaporate while establishing obvious distances from the referred textual sources. Unless you know these people outside of their textual figurations, you know them—like we know Briony—only in the detachment of writing. And like Briony these figures are dependent on an artifact of signified connections that itself composes a space of determinate options.

Optional in the sense that everything about them could have been changed by rewriting and in the further sense that when the document in which they appear disappears they too disappear. Except, perhaps, for a few fragile memories for a brief time. In my opinion, these narrators make a decisive difference for this chapter, but their appearances are saturated nonetheless by groundless indifference.

These narrators also serve to allow me to maintain a detachment in this chapter from the texts of which they speak. It is, after all, a chapter on neutral liberty; and although that liberty would have characterized any interpretation I might have given of Plato or Hume, for example, the increased distance from those texts in the figure of four other narrators might make more evident the chapter's subject matter (as McEwan's narrator, Briony, makes more evident the indifference that conditions Briony's-McEwan's "final act of kindness").

THE EXPERIENCE OF FREEDOM

Jean-Luc Nancy speaks of "essential" freedom as distinct to freedoms that individuals may enjoy.[6] I will avoid that phrase as I turn to his work, for reasons that will be apparent, although I believe there is an important distinction to make between freedoms and freedom. "Freedom" has so many meanings! To choose one sense of "freedom" like "indifferent freedom," and to talk about it, does not necessarily rule out the legitimacy of other meanings for the word. To be authoritarian about the meaning of freedom would lose freedom's meaning.

"Indifferent freedom" suggests in the context of this discussion a lack of necessary fixation, allowance of change, neutrality among options, release of restrictions and dominations. The phrase here suggests such allowance and release as simultaneous with the appearance—the manifest existence—of determinate restrictions. Nancy's account of the experience of freedom with the experience of whatever appears allows us to bring together senses of freedom, allowance, and indifference, especially with reference to singularity and communal life.

The site (he sometimes says "home") of freedom, as Nancy uses the word, is at the limit of understanding where existence begins. "Where existence begins" means where living events are manifest in their existence before they are represented or recognized as something, where the sheer "fact" of existence takes place. It is where thoroughly concrete and living rela-

6. Jean-Luc Nancy, *The Experience of Freedom,* trans. Bridget McDonald (Stanford, Calif.: Stanford University Press, 1993).

tions occur, where whatever comes to presence is, and where, for example, Briony's neatly formulated abstractions were obliterated by living, unruly events. As Nancy thinks of it, freedom is the property or characteristic of nothing. The word names the manifest occurrence of living things. Freedom does not happen as conceptual or intuitional structure, but it does happen as the existing eventuation of structures. It seems to require definitions, but its definitions require their own removal. Freedom, in fact, is at a remove from any representation, any imposition of meaning, image, or sense. It is exposure to the singular existences of things. For Nancy, freedom is simply and factually its own event. It happens as the exposure we undergo in our lives and to whatever lives in the environment.

"Exposure" in this context suggests the possibility of meaning. The happening of lives, as distinct from worldly, specific identities that happen, is free. The happening allows all manner of references and senses. It allows, in fact, for as many identifications as the worldly formation of a happening makes possible: This blue bottle in this kitchen with its limited history, intersecting with the histories and lives of those who live in and with this kitchen, in this city, in this culture . . . this bottle is limited and identified in its specific happening, and also available for many kinds of experiences and significances. But its free happening lets it go in being, as it were. It provides availability and seems both to remand the bottle to its own specificity and appearance and to release it to its disappearance at the borders of its existence. Freedom as Nancy thinks of it happens without limit as limited things happen, and it is obliquely apparent in fragmentation, singularity, cessation, disappearance, coming to presence, borders, and wandering.

Another way of speaking of freedom (that, in fact, will not be comprehended) is to say that it is manifest in a differenciating way at the cusp of living differences and ideas or objects. Things are unleashed in their differences, by virtue of *their* existence. Freedom is differential in the sense that singular beings *happen* singularly, and unleashing in this context means the instability of the limits that define them, their capacity to cease being what they are, their freedom with recognitions that would hold them. It means their finitude, the limits of their existence, their limits in existing. Things slip away; freedom is slippage from determinations. Slippage, continuous slippage among all singular things. That's one way to speak of our common freedom; we are together in common, not because of controlling determinations—such determinations establish noncommonality, juxtapositions, divergence. We are together in common by virtue of indeterminate freedom and the slippage in determinations that we share. Existence in freedom composes our commonality.

One of Nancy's strategies is to follow various concepts of freedom, including his own, until what they are about—freedom—seems manifest in the concept's insufficiency. He speaks of "the fragmentation of a thinking of freedom." "Consequently," he says, "freedom cannot be signaled except as that which comes to thought only through the 'agony' of this thought, with the 'strangling' of this discourse. . . . In speaking of freedom one has to accept being confronted by this insistent stripping away" (149). The experience of freedom continues in the incompetence of its thought and the inadequacy of the words used in its regard. It is not an end to be sought or even a possible destination. It happens in the appearing of things, in efforts to think it or say it, in the lives of those attempts, in what we might call living thoughts and discourse. It is always apart—severe in its detachment—in its determinate location, in the spaces of fragmented ideas and interrupted phrases. The experience of freedom is found in its insistent loss of specific location, in the specific locations of its occurrence.

People share this enticement and loss of freedom. It's as though something were always lost or incomplete, as though freedom's slippage makes every determinate order a fragment of difference among differences. We share freedom's enticement and loss as we make freedom dependent on definitive commitments and properly regulated lives, as we experience the limits of authoritative structures—as we *authoritatively* come up against the limits and know that we will have to protect and defend the borders again and again, as though such protection would make us free. We experience freedom as we live with borders that open out to no order as well as to other borders, as we know vaguely no-border coming with borders. We experience freedom as we dream Briony's dream of an unfragmented continuity of order and purpose, as we undergo the failure of abstractions and holistic imagery, as we insist on unity without end. And we experience freedom also when we think not so much *about* it, but rather when we think it—when we think freedom as thought is freed from its own necessary limits. Then we might find that we need but cannot keep the limits, that we must lose them and find them again, reborn. Freedom is shared, Nancy says, even when we do not know it. Existence happens with singular, living things, with failed attempts at sufficient knowledge, with dominations and liberties. And wherever existence happens, freedom and its loss take place.

Nancy's thought of freedom as "exposure to the limit" allows—I doubt that he would use Annette Baier's term "careless philosophy," but he could use a complementary phrase like "fragmentary strictness" to emphasize the rigor he needs to write in resonance with freedom's differencial nonpresence (148ff.). This strictness demands attention to singular occurrences in the context of a fragmented world. It—this strictness—composes an attunement to freedom; it composes a singular disposition. In Nancy's instance I believe it comprises a love of freedom. He finds himself inclined to hold its slippage in mind, to understand himself and others in the experience of freedom, to know that the institutions of freedom will fail, that he (we) can carry out a love of freedom only by letting it be free. That means, at least, attention to the optional quality—the freedom—of values, meanings, and truths, in their affirmation and pursuit, a relentless strictness with passions that push toward dominance and immediate certainties, a rigor of restraint with the lives of whatever lives. This attunement does not promise much beyond continuous effort to find ways to affirm freedom and to avoid its destruction. A first step is in learning how to think and affirm without an overwhelming sense of determinate grounding and with a sense of free eventuation. Until that happens our affirmations, values, and programs— our impatience to institute justice—will probably work against freedom and will eventuate in yet more scaffolding that figures suppression of freedom while appearing to confirm it.

VARIATION

Clive Linley needed a small variation in the last movement of his score.[7] He had almost completed his commissioned Millennium Symphony.

> All that was required now was to go back several pages in the score to the clamorous restatement and vary the harmonies, perhaps, or even the melody itself, or devise some form of rhythmic undertow, a syncopation that cut into the leading edge of the notes. To Clive, this variation had become a crucial feature of the work's conclusion; it needed to suggest the future's un-knowability. When that by now familiar melody returned for the very last time, altered in a small and significant way, it should prompt insecurity in the listener; it was a caution against clinging too tightly to what he knew. (146–47)

It would complete a momentous and beautiful work.

The melody that he wanted to vary had come to him in the form of a bird's call while he was hiking. He had been waiting for it for weeks and took a hiking vacation in the hope that a change of pace and scenery would provide relaxation and distraction and allow the crucial few notes to come to him that would tie the symphony together and make it memorable and beautiful. It was those few notes of melody that he wanted to vary enough to announce the millennial change. His strategy of getting away and hiking had worked. When he heard the bird call high above the upland plateau he knew that he had the clue to what he was searching for. The melody and

---

7. Ian McEwan, *Amsterdam* (New York: Anchor Books, 1999).

harmony began to sound for him "an inversion of a line he had already scored for a piccolo. How elegant, how simple. Turning the sequence round opened up the idea of a plain and beautiful song in common time, which he could almost hear. But not quite" (90).

He needed to get it down before the faint sound in his mind, like the bird, soared beyond perception. "He heard it, he had it, then it was gone. There was a glow of a tantalizing afterimage and the fading call of a sad little tune. This symphony was a torment" (91). He had reached for his notebook and pencil. He was able to follow the afterglow thanks only to immediate concentration: The momentous last movement, the final testament to the twentieth century and its passage, could now be prepared throughout the great work, brought to its ending, and given just enough variation to begin to slip away into another time. He was able to concentrate, standing by a rock on Allen Cragis in the Highlands, and recall the melody. But his inspiration for the variations in their integration into the score several weeks later was irrevocably interrupted, and his music went to Amsterdam for its inauguration in the Concertgebouw without it. "Fatally unvaried" (173). This variation "should have been the symphony's moment of triumphant assertion, the gathering up of all that was joyously human before the destruction to come. But presented like this [without variation], as simple fortissimo repetition, it was literal-minded bombast, it was bathos, less than that, it was a void: one that only revenge could fill." "The theme was disintegrating into the tidal wave of dissonance" (173). Clive Linley was not made for an aesthetics of dissonance. Or for the drone into which his music descended without the variation.

The melody had made its transition from elusive fantasy to notes in his notebook because of a decision Clive made in the Highlands. As he was beginning to write down the fragment of sound running precariously through his brain, he heard distant voices. Against his better judgment he peered over the top of the rock in whose protection he was writing in his notebook—the melody that was taking shape had to do with "an optimistic resolve against odds, courage" (91)—and saw below him some thirty feet a man and a woman. Perhaps an assignation. He returned to his notebook until the woman's voice became shrill and he could not ignore it. He looked again. The woman was struggling to resist the man's aggression. The melody —the symphony—was in the balance. Any further distraction would surely erase the arising order of notes, the birth of "the lamented century's ode to joy," its musical culmination (94). As the man's aggression turned to unambiguous violence, Clive made a decision: He walked quickly away, preserving for a few more moments his memory of the unwritten notes. He found a flat rock out of the reach of the woman's distressed cries and scribbled the crucial signs. He knew they could not have survived even a mild distraction, much less an intensely disturbing one. The millennium could now come into its aesthetic own.

In fact, the woman was the victim of a serial rapist. She escaped, but many other women did not, including one victim after Clive's decision. The rapist was arrested. One of Clive's friends reported (against Clive's will) to the police that Clive had witnessed the events, and as he was about to pen the crucial variation into the larger work, no less fragile an undertaking than the melody's inspiration, the police arrived to require his immediate presence in their office in Manchester. His concentration was destroyed—he had no choice in this matter. He had to send his terribly late score to the British Symphony before he left for Manchester and after he lost the notes and his auditory vision for the completed work. He died of poisoning in Amsterdam a few days later (where he had gone for the first presentation of his work) before he could change the failed last movement. He was the victim of fatal revenge. He also, with revenge, poisoned his former friend: "literal-minded bombast . . . bathos . . . a void: one that only revenge could fill" (173). Those words describe not only his recognition of the symphony's last movement but also his own self-absorbed life. And, likely, the twentieth century as well.

I recount this story because it allows an elaboration of the element of variation in one kind of experience of freedom—a variation on the theme of variation, if you will. And it also tells of a remarkable choice that confronts Clive in a moment of significant creativity. A double responsibility presented itself: responsibility to a suffering victim of violence and that to the creation of something beautiful. Here is a play of variations with moral goodwill and a creator's untimely opportunity to occasion a new and culturally upbuilding event. The factors of variation and the indefiniteness of a process of metamorphosis are as insistent here as in Briony's quandary over variations in her conclusion to her virtual history of real events. How is one to choose with so many variations happening in a formation of textured experience? How might we make a whole cloth—a whole score—of an experience when experience is so varied in the clash and impact of so many demanding events? Nonresolution? An experience of freedom's indifference?

Had Clive completed the variations and had his Millennium Symphony become a genuinely great work of genius (one that lifted thousands of spirits and gave them to soar), would his indifference on Allen Cragis find justification? Clive thought so. He was completely absorbed in his work—like Beethoven, Haydn, and Bach. But he found himself far from being a master of variation. He lived in the oscillation of energy generated by self-delusion and exceptional, recognized talent. His life revolved around a limited capacity for love and genuine creative talent, around a need for undisturbed solitude and the requirements of professional organization and citizenship. His decisive indifference to the woman's life during his hike arose from the demands of creative work as well as from complete attachment to his own work. I imagine that he maintained resonance with the indifference of variations, the very dimension of his music's theme. He could have affirmed the liberty required to leave his score and turn to the woman's distress. The banality and self-preoccupation reflected in his choice seem to me to show a lack of detachment from his work that departing from it suddenly would require. His is a failure of overdetermination. But how was he, energized and dedicated as he was in his restricted character, to know? Isn't he a cipher of dissonant variations in his twentieth-century culture? A figure of profound heedlessness and insensibility due to overcommitment? A person of his time in a conclusive play of demands and attachments?[8]

Perhaps in another telling he would have rushed to help the woman. Perhaps the attacker would have pushed him into the nearby tarn, causing his notebook to fall out of his pocket as he struggled in his heavy clothes and boots. His notes might have been lost forever. Perhaps the event would have given birth to a new and greater final movement for his symphony, making it a genuine masterpiece. Perhaps Clive would have been killed. Or he might have heroically succeeded in protecting the woman. There is too much distance, too much freedom, too much inconclusiveness to know.

The open space of storytelling gives us no more answers than the freedom of existence does. Freedom is indifferent, but in our differences we are not. Experiences of beauty, revenge, generosity, largeness of spirit can make significant differences. How do we measure the relative weight of the sacrifices required by situations of variations? Is it a spiritual failure on Clive's part that makes his refusal to help the woman indefensible? Would it have

---

8. I wonder about the revenge that McEwan appears to take on Clive—his failed symphony, his vapid revenge, his death. Is McEwan's revenge an indication of a lack of nobility? Another sensibility, Briony's, for example, might have allowed Clive to complete his variations and to write a great symphony, and thereby present a greater quandary because of his genuine quality and aesthetic success. As the story is told, however, the century ends—too late for integration—with compounded cowardice, manipulation, banality, selfishness, deception, sickness, and murder. The story's own spirit seems lost in its details, and although its readers will know of spiritual oblivion, they cannot be sure on the basis of the story what has been lost. McEwan's irony and dark humor provide relief from the manifest weakness and insipidity. Perhaps the indifference of showing what it shows is enough. "Amoral" was Briony's word. *Amsterdam* has more sardonic laughter and judgment than *Atonement*. On the other hand, it does present a quandary that I believe many creative and productive people face, and one that can intensify the experience of freedom's indifference. I wonder, however, whether it is too attached to the century's failures, to its banality, to appreciate fully the liberty of indifference.

been defensible if his music, consequent to ignoring her call for help, elevated people's spirits and provided a moving experience of beauty and insight, an expression of the spiritual nobility that our culture so needs? Or the reverse: Would it have been defensible if he had helped the woman and lost a symphony's beauty?

I expect that living with such questions—*that* attunement with indifferent freedom—makes an important difference in the ways we live together, that Clive's failure is found in his attached sense of rightness and lack of question, in choosing as he did. Basic moral certainty and clarity have their greatest danger in self-assurance, when we know the fundamental answers and look only for the means of their application. It seems that the virtue of clear decisiveness is *a part* of free variations and that to ignore the freedom of variability in our clarity of determination verges on banal conclusiveness and a lack of rigor in attention to the detachment of indifferent freedom.

The dangers are that we in our decisiveness lose alertness to the lives, the free lives, that we intend to determine with justice and goodness, as well as that we lose our bearings and our decency in indecisiveness. In either case, we are in danger of losing a variable and vital sense of being free. The problem that Clive presents is one of strength and decisiveness: He made a clear choice in his field of commitment. He wanted a conclusion appropriate to his project. He lacked the distance provided by attunement to indifferent freedom, and in his attachment perhaps he did indeed exemplify one of his culture's major failings.

SEVERITY WITHOUT COMPLETION

Experiences of indifferent freedom are not always severe. They sometimes comprise reveries of opening and release, as though one were unconfined by definitive boundaries. Often they promise possibilities of liberation from what would appear without them as necessities. Usually they suggest optionality, variability, never fixation. But these experiences can also bring with them a sense of severity and incompleteness, especially when they accompany losses of valuable lives or a dominance of cruelty and evil—most particularly when those losses and dominations come with beauty. When we experience pronounced presence, beauty and indifference with barbarity, injustice, or other violent occurrences, freedom can appear severe—not severe with judgment but severe in its lack of care or countenance, in its seeming radiance of pure unconcern. Things happen—come to presence—with nothing to hold them except the determinations that define them, encompass them, let them live, nurture them, injure them, or kill them. Indifferent freedom appears severe as things struggle to be as they are, severe in its lack of struggle, preference, determination. How might such severity come to articulation?

Robinson Jeffers.[9] His poetry is often austere, severe, hard. In comparison to his Asian friend's mysticism, he says that his poetry is "harder" as he responds with things, that things happen as they are, excessive to any work of the mind, outside of its comprehension:

> The water is the water, the cliff is the rock, come shocks and flashes of
> reality. The mind
> Passes, the eye closes, the spirit is a passage;
> The beauty of things was born before eyes and sufficient to itself; the
> heart-breaking beauty
> Will remain when there is no heart to break for it.[10]

Consider his poem "Apology for Bad Dreams" (part I, p. 141):

> In the purple light, heavy with redwood, the slopes drop seaward,
> Headlong convexities of forest, drawn in together to the steep ravine.
> Below, on the sea cliff,
> A lonely clearing; a little field of corn by the streamside; a roof under
> spared trees. Then
> the ocean
> Like a great stone someone has cut to a sharp edge and polished to shining,
> Beyond it, the fountain
> And furnace of incredible light flowing up from the sunk sun. In the
> little clearing
> a woman
> Is punishing a horse; she had tied the halter to a sapling at the edge of the
> wood, but
> when the great whip,
> Clung to the flanks the creature kicked so hard she feared
> He would snap the halter; she called from the house
> the young man, her son; who fetched a chain tie-rope, they working
> together
> Noosed the small rusty links round the horse's tongue.
> And tied him by the swollen tongue to the tree.

---

9. Jeffers says of poetry: "As presenting the universal beauty poetry is an incitement to life; an incitement to action, because our actions are part of the beauty; an incitement to contemplation, because it serves to open our intelligence and senses to that beauty." "Credo," from *The Selected Poetry of Robinson Jeffers,* ed. Tim Hunt (Stanford, Calif.: Stanford University Press, 2001), 38.

10. *Selected Poetry of Robinson Jeffers,* 147.

Seen from this height they are shrunk to insect size,
Out of all human relation. You cannot distinguish
The blood dripping from where the chain is fastened,
The beast shuddering; but the thrust neck and the legs
Far apart. You can see the whip fall on the flanks . . .
The gesture of the arm. You cannot see the face of the woman.
The enormous light beats up out of the west across
The cloud-bars of the trade-wind. The ocean
Darkens, the high clouds brighten, the hills darken
    together. Unbridled and unbelievable beauty
Covers the evening world . . . not covers, grows apparent
    out of it, as Venus down there grows out
From the lit sky. What said the prophet? "I create good:
    and I create evil: I am the Lord."[11]

---

11. *Selected Poetry of Robinson Jeffers,* 141.

SEVEN

In the Name of Goodness

In short, I am full of doubts. I really don't know why I have
decided to pluck up my courage and present, as if it were
authentic, the manuscript of Adso of Melk. Let us say it
is an act of love. Or, if you like, a way of ridding myself of
numerous, persistent obsessions. I transcribe my text with no
concern for timeliness. In the years when I discovered the
Abbe Vallet volume, there was a widespread conviction that
one should write only out of a commitment to the present,
in order to change the world. Now, after ten years or more,
the man of letters (restored to his highest dignity) can
happily write out of pure love of writing. And so I now
feel free to tell, for sheer narrative pleasure, the story of
Adso of Melk, and I am comforted and consoled in finding
it immeasurably remote in time (now that the waking of
reason has dispelled all the monsters that its sleep had
generated), gloriously lacking in any relevance for our day,
atemporally alien to our hopes and our certainties.

—Umberto Eco, *The Name of the Rose*

All sorrows can be borne if we put them in a story
or tell a story about them.

—Isak Dinesen

Well, the last chapter certainly ended on a note of abruptness and severity! I want to make accessible for thought the dimension of form-
less indifference that we cannot apprehend in a comprehensive way. We
must think without grasping—that is the point, I believe, when we consider indifferent freedom. There is a dimension of occurrence that will not
happen as grasped or as held by intentional forms such as concepts or objects of desire. It's severe in holding apart from human cares and determi-

nations. The distance and detachment that it composes in experience seem to allow for impermanence in our most intense figurations of conviction and knowledge, to allow for the distance of radical variations and transformations as well as for repetition, uncertainty, and transfiguring recreation. We have seen the play of indifference in certain experiences of beauty, "soul," composition, and obligation. I turn now to questions about goodness in the context of indications of indifference in the meaning of the word. This is a dimension of indifference that points out the danger of generalizing a group of goods and making it into a normative sense of goodness. When the indifference factor is left out, goodness appears to be in danger of becoming a name for oppressive and often-blind violence.

The word *goodness,* like the word *nature,* carries a huge burden. Both words suggest orders of highly diverse things. They can suggest the availability of systematic comprehension and articulation of those things they name, a common quality that allows at least the promise of a harmonious whole. "Goodness" often operates in its meaning on an axis of virtues and sustained social practices. The meaning of the word seems to intend a community that is organized by right values, that is, by goods. It would be a community that carries a sense of goodness, a community enacted in the name of goodness.

"Goodness" means the quality of being good. "Good," however, has so many senses that *a* sense of goodness is in jeopardy from the start. "Good" can mean a favorable character as well as profitable (a good deal). It means virtuous (a good person) as well as large in quantity (they won by a good margin). It can mean fertile (a good field) or conforming to a standard (good English). As a noun it can name something that conforms to a moral order or, in the plural, merchandise. It can mean proof of wrongdoing (she didn't have the goods on them) or forever (gone for good); net gain (ten bucks to the good) or certain kinds of people (the good).

"Goodness," on the other hand, does not generally mean the quality of fertility, profitability, or proof of wrongdoing, and although I plan to emphasize the problems raised by variety and differentiation among goods, I would like to restrict the sense of goodness to a context of moral virtues. We will also note that "goodness" has an overtone of eliciting a specific result, as in the phrase "good for a laugh," or good for the happiness of this group of people. But on the whole we will pay attention to the quality manifest in just and commendable conduct and in tendencies to a favorable character. I also want to hold in mind that in its Sanskrit origin "goodness" connotes the quality of holding fast.

The burden of "goodness," then, is found in its naming a quality that specifies the sense or meaning of moral commonality in the midst of many diverging practices and forces. It names a qualitative identity that persists in many situations and times, a persistence that means constancy, a constancy of connections among diverse goods. Further, "goodness" names a discernible quality that allows for interconnected or systematic comprehension, for an intelligent design that spawns articulate rationalities based on goodness. In short, in its force of naming a quality, "goodness" gives a certain authoritative and positive power to goods as well as a negative power or value to non-goods or anti-goods. It allows for procedures of sorting things out according to their definitive qualities. It provides a stable point of reference for recognition and judgment, for ordering behaviors and attitudes, for guidance in educating and correcting.

The power of a name like goodness is also found as a force of singularization. When people appear in their goodness, they stand out as this good one like other good ones who share the same quality in their singular characters. Goodness is in this case recognized as an intrinsic quality, not as on the surface, as it were, but indwelling the good ones. There are certainly behaviors that are good for something, and there are people who are good in the sense that they are skilled at what they do or who help in the progress of a larger purpose. But a morally good person or morally good actions are at the very least good in their singular happening due to *their* goodness. It's as though they happen *in* the name of goodness.

In its quality of goodness, morally good behavior is thus characterized by both order and singularity: singularity in the sense that goodness happens in a person's specific actions and way of living, and order in the sense that goods are discernibly interconnected in an accountable manner. At best, morally good behavior and attitudes would characterize a body of people who, like those in a well-trained chorus or schooled in ritual performances, find their satisfaction in disciplined repetitions of goodness and who are able to override those inclinations and emotions that would carry them away from the order of goodness. A positive sense of goodness brings people to order and defines good individuals.

Repetition seems necessary in singularized movements of goodness. The need for fine-tuning in new and different experiences, coping with the apparently unremitting forces of forgetfulness, meanness, foolishness, self-absorption, and transforming perspectives: The re-birth of goodness in constantly changing situations requires its repetition, its re-adaptation, its repeated affirmation if lives are to continue to be good. Goodness appears to be dependent on recognition—re-cognition—if its ordering sense is to remain forceful. It requires re-membering—replication—for its endurance in the stretch of times and circumstances.

Its dependence on recognition poses problems for the quality of goodness. There is no certainty that recognitions of goodness will be thoroughly under *its* governance, because recognitions are themselves composed of many diverse factors, such as the chaotic ambiguity of language, the often subtle and pervasive influence of powerful interests, and the impact of aggressive behaviors, practices, and attitudes. Such factors can produce perverse qualities opposed to goodness, as well as dilute and weaken its force.

Goodness is vulnerable to so many powers in the power of its own recognized definition and sensibility! Who will preserve its force? Who will speak and act for it? Who will stand for its authority? Who will hold firm to goodness?

The good, of course, will do their best. To preserve and keep established orders of goodness they might form schools; special signs and calendars; groups of the committed; sites for retreat, renewal, and remembrance; specially constituted libraries and curricula; institutes; guides for parents; bodies of authoritative writings; disciplines of practice; and systems of enforcement. Given the vulnerability of those orders, vigilance and careful education are crucial. Distraction and disintegration seem to be constant in the orders of goodness and especially at the margins of the values where their power fades out. Not only does disorder characterize the lives of the good in the forces of desire, self-interest, laziness, and historical formations of meaning, strong orders of goodness seem also to engender curiosity before non-good differences, to give rise to interest, even intense interest in what is not governed by goodness. Not to mention the emotions of love that are overwhelmed by certain singularities and that overthrow the goodness of wisdom and moral practice, as though in the performance of a great choir a tenor begins to sing a different song.

The story of goodness that I have told so far, however, refers to it in terms of a dominant system of virtues and their practice. The narrative is captivated by an image of a defining order, as though dominant moral practices constituted a prerogative for interpreting and articulating goodness, as though the privileges of powerful virtues included outlawing or banishing contrary values. Clearly there are regions where certain goods rule. In fact, there are many such regions and subregions, from families and communes to local organizations, to states and cultures. Usually, I imagine, there are clusters of different goods in all moral orders, struggles for power and movements of deviation. Far from a universal system of goods, there are huge moral differences in which one people's virtues are another's vices. When we consider goodness by reference to different moral systems or oppositions active within such orders, the image of *a* system of goodness seems absurd. Goodness appears rather more as an abstract category that is available for determination by contradictory, shaping social forces. Viewed this way, goodness seems to be indifferent to the authority of any regional grouping. It appears as a powerful category that is on hand for the justification of radically opposed ways of life. As the quality or state of being good, goodness is accessible to any group that has the power to name what is good and what is bad. Goodness doesn't seem to intend any one set that authorizes itself in the name of goodness.

Such indifference can lead us to hope that goodness names something discoverable and "natural," something in our hearts and minds, no matter how deeply hidden, or in the very nature of living events or in a physical order in the universe. Perhaps nature itself tends toward a grand and good unity and for unknown reasons is having a hard time getting there. Or, if not nature, the human spirit—something in human nature that strives for the quality of goodness and in its time will come to a recognition of what is truly good and truly bad. Perhaps "goodness" names a natural reality, in some way like a being, something properly called goodness itself. Outside of hopes and interpretations, however, we have little evidence for such a reality, and we face ourselves and our lineages repeatedly in the images of "natural entities" by which we variously cast the unity of people and things. The abstract indifference of goodness seems blandly to house those images along with so many others, to slip into many histories and senses, to have an availability that only *absence* of nature and identity enjoys.

This is not such a good story I'm telling in the sense that it isn't especially upbuilding. It doesn't seem to be conforming to a standard of virtue; *if* it tends toward the formation of favorable character, the tendency is very retiring; whether it is even salutary is not at all clear. It seems to undercut the authority, even the value of goodness. If I understand this narrative correctly, it does not support goodness even as a desirable good. What's the point?

Let's think about desire for goodness.

DESIRE FOR GOODNESS

I assume that most people we know want to be good in some sense, to have a share of goodness, as it were. More than recognition that they are good, most people we know probably want to feel good about themselves, to enjoy a sense of personal integrity and accomplishment, and to feel integrated with what they find good in their environment. That doesn't mean that they all want the same thing or what we recognize as a salutary character or that they want to be skilled in what we know as worthwhile pursuits. What appears good to them might appear defiant or illegal to us or selfish or just plain wrong. They might be good party members of parties we find bad, or hold fast to values we consider irresponsible. But at the end of the day (and with many exceptions, I am sure), most people we know probably feel a desire to respect themselves in their goodness and to be a good part of some social order. The desire to be good, in other words, can be a desire that is fulfilled by what we think of as perverse and by orders of behavior that we judge to be radically immoral.

How might we interpret the desire to be good? As the faint voice of goodness, now in the image of something much greater than us, and specifically good? As a natural drift toward spiritual maturation and ultimate exposure of the perversity of hindrances to such growth? Is the quality of goodness really—in fact—a sign of something elemental in life, or perhaps more than a sign, a participant in a force of goodness that exceeds human comprehension? As good, are we in the flow of such purposeful excess? And they, the not-good, is their devious flow to be corrected in the name of goodness? Wars have been fought over smaller stakes, but I suppose if we're on the side of goodness and want to be good by holding fast to it, we should do all we can to convert or at least restrain those who fight against what we most virtuously want.

My unhappiness over those interpretive options arises from the observation that the desire to be good, like goodness in this respect, is not under the jurisdiction of any specific group of virtues. This desire has more to do with perceptions of what is salutary in interconnected groups of lives than with states of nature or supratemporal worlds. Our desire to be good brings to expression an extensive lineage of physical development and moral practices. The immense and creative force of "goodness"—its value—has its own history of formation. I am unable to say whether the force of goodness carries the transvaluation of what was once bad and then, by weakness of spirit, became good (as Nietzsche has it). I expect, however, that the rise and fall of various goods in their dominating force has less to do with willpower, that, indeed, desire has less to do with willpower than Nietzsche thought. Desires appear to arise with a considerable amount of chemical and genetic information as well as with formations that originate in structures of punishment, repression and encouragement, cultural sensibility, and thoroughly appropriated manners of life and belief. Desire thus appears to arise, not from a greater desire or conscious purposes, but from biological and cultural elements that together figure something different, something other to chemicals, genes, and social influences, something by the name of desires that we embody and translate in our singular lives. Desires do not tell us much about things other than themselves and the lineages they carry, and when we break them down into their component parts, we do not have much to go on other than the parts and their organization, much less a foundation for them. Desires, like clouds, rise to their glory, reflecting much that is around them, and then dissipate, leaving a wake, certainly, but not for long.

TRANSLATING GOODNESS

From one angle of observation, I have been addressing the translation of a sense of goodness by means of textures of goods. *Translation* suggests to carry across an interval or divide, to transfer something or to move it definitively into a different being. Something that is translated, whether a word or a person, never remains unchanged. Translation persistently and strangely opens up differences—opens *out* to differences—in efforts to establish sameness of meaning. It brings with it slippage and departure as well as communication and connection. Translation is different from simple repetition. It seems to carry with it something unrepeatable, something adrift and yet transferred and transmuted in a translational occurrence. Or at least it does on favorable translation days when, by translation, we encounter traces of what is translated in its difference from what is representably before us.

Deeds and affections in the name of goodness, especially when they are viewed by reference to their conflicting and uncountable differences, appear to translate a sense of goodness; they appear as goods and transfer to various circumstances that qualitative sense. I have said that an untranslatable indifference seems to come with the differences that goods make, and I have interpreted such indifference by reference to the ubiquity of goodness in its sense and force, the seeming indifference of its name to its many and often opposing translations. It's almost as though "goodness" named a transcendent force of life, although it appears on close inspection to be rather more like a powerful name with all the rights and privileges that powerful names have.

A DOUBTFUL OPTION

Many people in our culture, I expect, are reasonably aware of the excesses occasioned by passions for certain values: deception and guile in the name of "higher" goods, honesty that hides ambiguities, narrow and destructive commitments, we/they structures in connecting with people, and enflamed righteousness, to name a few. And we know the terrible damage that a lack of passion for values can bring: carelessness before suffering, silence in the presence of oppression, self-absorption and unwillingness to serve the interest of other people, detachment from the travail of things. On the one hand, people's intense desire that something be so—that their sense of justice, for example, rule their society or that all people enjoy a democratic form of government—can wreak havoc in their simple and straight-arrow invocation of justice and democracy. On the other hand, people without imaginative passion, without visions of improved lives, can look for pockets of security and allow havoc its sway. Is there anything more important or more dangerous than human goodness? More decisive or more destructive than human commitments? More in question than "human" and "goodness"? Wherever there is a "we" the name of goodness seems to operate, as though being a "we" were goodness in itself.

In the epigraph of this chapter I quote the translator and editor of the Italian version of an obscure, neo-Gothic French version of a seventeenth-century Latin edition of a work written in Latin by a German monk toward the end of the fourteenth century.[1] This anonymous translator carries out his scholarly work beginning in the tumultuous year, 1968, when Eastern and Western Europe underwent a considerable political upheaval. It was also a time of considerable personal upset for the author. He decided to transcribe from notes and sketchy sources into modern Italian a narrative purportedly written by Adso of Melk in the fourteenth century, providing a sense of continuity and contemporaneity that falsify the translator's own doubts about the uncertain and broken quality of his sources. My reasons for including the epigraph are these: The author tells a story by translation; he says that it is written with no sense for its timeliness; he identifies the time of his writing as one during which many people write out of virtuous, political commitments to ethical relevance; he identifies his own motivation as narrative pleasure, a pleasure he takes in Adso's perplexed and ordered account of a labyrinthine mystery that takes place in a labyrinthine library filled with apocalyptic symbolism, a library that is destroyed by an apocalyptic fire caused by a blind sense of goodness; this narrative, in contrast to Eco's *Foucault's Pendulum,* is chronologically straightforward and uses its apparent temporal and narrative exactness of order to heighten the irony in presenting an order of goodness that destroys a repository of learning as well as curiosity and heartfelt laughter. The translator, I think, takes pleasure in presenting a labyrinth that is like the labyrinth of both translation and the lineage of this translation. It is a pleasure that leads to laughter in presenting an extremely serious dedication to an order of goodness. The narrative, in its apparent and pleased indifference to political and moral relevance, enjoys many levels of good humor as well as sorrow as it speaks of the self-destruction of a specific order of goodness. Its pleasure and neutrality in the telling of highly partisan conflicts allow a region where the kinds of goods that it describes have no jurisdiction. It allows nonpartisan distance and a quality of resonance, empathy, and imaginative play but not a clear sense of goodness.

A relief takes place in the book's irrelevant pleasure, offsetting the awful sobriety inspired by an overheated sense of goodness and offsetting also a

---

1. Umberto Eco, *The Name of the Rose* (New York: Warner Books, 1980).

contemporary, overheated desire for relevance that is probably in the direct lineage of the earlier sobriety. It's not that the narrative is good (or bad). It's that it releases an almost indifferent quality of enjoyment, an option to carelessness and to a sense of goodness as well, a pleasure that seems congruent with the indifference that is lost to translations of goodness into intensely desired goods. This relief takes place as a narrative freedom, a special opening to stories of conflict without an imperative to dominate the conflicts, stories of impassioned quests and self-protective organizations, but stories that do not require poetic justice or an uplifting moral. This narrative intention of freedom that incorporates a sensibility of pleasure in telling, writing, discovering, and inventing is surely a doubtful option to the multiple passions whose stories it tells, a doubtful option to moral seriousness. But the force of this freedom—its valence, its value—provides an atmosphere that allows for something other than the kinds of desire that have dominated many of our moral traditions. It allows for attitudes and values formed in the recognized slippage of translations and the foolishness of many moral conflicts, and it provides an opening to transmutations of what we often think of as moral commitments in the name of goodness. This freedom allows for growth of freedom, for an unfolding of free space, and, perhaps, for ways of life that hold in question the powerful name of goodness.

I would like to consider one instance of such transmutation.

DAVID WOOD ON REVENGE

I am speaking of transformations of attitudes and contexts for recognition when I speak of this pleasure in translating Adso's piecemeal narrative about a clash among "the good." It includes a shift in the narrative's world from virtuous commitment to a presentation of such commitment outside the jurisdiction of the commitment. Adso remained a good Dominican even as he transcribed the strange events in the remote and now lost abbey. He tells a story that happens outside the reach of his commitments; his commitments are part of the story, but he does not attempt to understand the story on the basis of his own beliefs or those of the major characters. He *reports* his piety and faith rather than writing a document of faith. And the translator remains true to his task in the pleasure he takes in presenting an order—like a grammatical order—that houses radical and random absence of order.

The value of this kind of attitude—that of Adso's narrative and of the translator's, an attitude that has little to do with political and virtuous relevance, one that allows without comment a presentation of non-good disorders of disaster, an attitude that is able to culminate in laughter (to Adso's unresolved surprise as well as sorrow)—the valence and force of this kind of attitude are elaborated in Nietzsche's understanding of revenge. I would like to carry out this elaboration by noting David Wood's way of reading (his translation of) that understanding. Wood approaches Nietzsche's attitude toward revenge through Heidegger's transformation of Nietzsche's account of revenge against time. This is not a process of refutation but one of transformation that seems to have a significant and affirmative resonance with the finite quality of time. Instead of narration, we are turning to a way of thinking and a signifying structure that transforms Nietzsche's thought of revenge without taking revenge on it, transforms Nietzsche's thought in a way that also appropriates it. I find in this transformation an approximation to the narrative freedom found in *The Name of the Rose,* and that amounts to a translation, in Nietzsche's, Wood's, and Heidegger's instances, of a nonrepresentable dimension of time. It suggests a different ethos or way of life from that lived in the name of goodness.

The accent now falls on the aspect of Nietzsche's account of revenge that addresses the ways we experience and give order to time. "Revenge" takes place as people, in their dominant images and beliefs, defy inevitabilities in their lives, the continuous transformations of values and meanings, for example, or the perspectival limitations on knowledge and certainty. When we think of the past as completed in the sense that what happened has happened and cannot be changed, we are faced with another inevitability that accompanies conceptions of time as a series of completed nows: the inevitability that forward, transforming temporal movement is qualified by the petrification of the past. In this sense of inevitability, a deep hopelessness and heaviness seeps into human spiritedness, something like a preconscious sense of defeat by time—on the one hand, we are forever losing what we most prize, and on the other, the dead hand of the past clutches our spirit and squeezes life-force from it. In the consequent spirit of revenge, people lose motivation for genuine accomplishment, passionate curiosity, artistic creativity, and the discipline and fortitude that kind of living requires. We sink into repeated, moral platitudes, behaviors within easy range of accomplishment, cultivation of we-ish taste rather than unique deeds. We repeat our defeat as we order ourselves to defend what is ours and destroy differences that challenge us. Above all we require that indifferent time have meaning and purpose. You know the dreary consequences: societies of good and evil, thought by calculation and argument, simpleminded lies about the past and its harsh impact, and democracies authorized by the lowest common denominator in which excellence becomes the enemy; orders without *arête.* So does Nietzsche find revenge.

David Wood begins his discussion of revenge by considering the flow of repetition when Heidegger returns to Nietzsche's thought of revenge and rethinks it.[2] Heidegger returns to Nietzsche's thought to think *with* him and to follow his thought as much as he can in spite of a profound divergence on the question of temporality. One of his purposes is to engage an important and originary movement in Western philosophy, a trajectory of non-representational thinking in the West that Nietzsche brings to an original articulation in his conceptualization of revenge. Heidegger's engagement constitutes an exchange, an encounter *in* which thinking, as distinct to reportage, happens. It will be an encounter that is not reducible to either thinker's stance nor to a combination of their positions, nor to argument and refutation. It will be a determination of thought in a temporal movement of repetition in which something other to representable contents might be traced, "something," as it were, that seems to appear indirectly and in excess to representations. Wood uses the word *given* in this context: Something outside of representation is given or gives itself to be thought. Not a quality and not a conceptual truth, but time's occurrence, its dissolution of representability and of the dominance of meaning—in the language of this chapter, time's indifference and its strange force that translates repeatedly as the question *of* being deathly and living at the same time. Such an occurrence is similar to a conversation, the experience of which occasions a transformation for the participants, however slight, of the way they were or of what they knew or believed when the conversation began, a conversation that unfreezes past attitudes and practices and opens toward different behavior. If I were careful, I might be able to call such an experience a transference of what cannot be said directly but *appears* to be *traced* in the *life* of the exchange. And traced, perhaps, *only* in the exchange. On Heidegger's terms some people attempt to retrieve or recover such occurrences, not by imitating them or ritualizing their memory but by repeatedly engaging those philosophers whose thought is considerably in excess to what can be re-presented about their thought. The engagement is the site of transformation as well as of repetition, and if it's a good day for thinking, something of time will happen with reflective intensity that is not a matter of will or of objective knowledge but is a matter of release from the progenitors of revenge—a release, as Wood and Nietzsche and Heidegger have it, from that commonality that deeply fears the risks of time's transformative openings and departures.

Wood then engages Heidegger in Heidegger's retrieval of Nietzsche's thought of revenge. After noting Heidegger's appropriation of Nietzsche's showing that one kind of pervasive revenge arises from a sense of time as a

---

2. The following account is based on Wood's *Thinking after Heidegger* (Cambridge: Polity Press, 2002), 60–77.

series of nows in which the past appears as always lost, and after noting the limits of Heidegger's analysis and critical observations, Wood does some performative repeating of his own. He not only says *that* Heidegger's process of engaging Nietzsche "demonstrates" a "repetition of [Nietzsche's] singularity" by the way he rethinks the account of time that underlies Nietzsche's thought. He also shows that Heidegger returns to Nietzsche in a way that performs an overcoming of the experience of time that determines the spirit of revenge. As he shows that Heidegger's thought in the spirit of renewal turns beyond the force of revenge, Wood opens the way for a repetition of Heidegger's thought. It is a translational repetition and way of thought that are informed by Wood's engagements with thinkers after Heidegger, with Derrida above all but also with Levinas and many others. Wood's engagement with Heidegger is attuned to the way Heidegger's thought moves—to the way it *lives*—in its enactment, attuned to its performative and, I would add, translational dimension. And Wood brings thought in the aftermath of Heidegger's thought to bear in his retrieval of Heidegger, just as Heidegger brought thought after Nietzsche to bear in his return to Nietzsche. To Heidegger's thought of retrieval, in other words, Wood gives a transformational dimension that is informed by Derrida's and Levinas's translations of Heidegger's thought. That kind of retrieval is like Heidegger's retrieval of Nietzsche in the sense that something past is translated in the force of its aftermath into something that opens out to a nondetermined future. The retrieval is a repetition of an originary quality in thinking, of a disposition toward natality and new life that invests Western thought. That's "what" is traced: like a quality that will not happen as an object or representation.

So we have three aspects of retrieval going on at once: (1) Heidegger's retrieval of Nietzsche that Wood follows; (2) Nietzsche's retrieval of revenge in Western culture, a retrieval that Heidegger translates in the work that Wood brings forward; and (3) Wood's retrieval of Heidegger in a translation that comprises thinking in a lineage that comes after Heidegger. In all three instances the issue concerns a kind of vengefulness, a pattern of inflicting injury on lively events, a pattern that arises from a sense of time without attunement to the continuous opening out of time, its always providing translatability for events in their passage. Time's mortality gives possibility and transfiguration: Revenge as Nietzsche thinks of it arises out of a profoundly hampered sense of futurity, transformation, and death. And it is the transformation of this hampered sense that Wood finds in Heidegger's engagement with Nietzsche's thought. The transformation of the spirit of revenge also happens in the form and movement of Wood's retrieval of Heidegger. It's not correctness or the knockdown of Heidegger's or Nietzsche's thought by critical blows that really counts for thinking. It's encountering the *life* of a way of thinking, hearing it, experiencing it, carrying it forward by translational thinking, by a shift in the signifying structure that presents it, by the value of a different way of thinking that comes to itself and its order *in* the impact and forceful lineage of the thinking that undergoes translation. Above all, for Wood, what counts is paying attention to the transformative dimensions of thinking: because affirmation of continuing transformation composes a friendly environment, not a vengeful one, for the lives of thought as well as for the lives of other kinds of things. For Wood, it's as though time with its continuous transmutational futurity is at once a gift and a giver. The gift of time, when it is well thought, translates revenge into life-affirmation. He calls it a responsive relation to the impossibility of thorough completion. I add that it is also a responsive relation to a dimension of living that appears as neither good nor bad, but appears as indifferently else than goodness.

REVENGE AND GOODNESS

To say that goodness is bad would be absurd. The badness of goodness has not been the problem that I want to address in this chapter. "Goodness" names the problem. The problem is with a *sense* of the quality of being good. I have noticed particularly orders of goodness, the extreme diversity of goods and *their* orders. I have attributed ordering power to the name and sense of goodness, and I have interpreted the connection between the quality of being good and goods as one of translation in which the indifference of goodness is often lost. I have also said that in its ordering force in specific moral systems, in spite of its indifference to determinate content, and in its enmeshment with the desire to be good, goodness appears to inspire systems of obedience and conformity as well as violence. Violence arises as people attempt to gain sole ownership of the rights to goodness's translation. The validity and right of various ways of life seem to depend on such ownership. All manner of bads are spawned in knowledge and recognition controlled by these possessive good mores. Goodness is not bad; it's rather as though it were a good *thing*, as though it were *a* difference instead of merely a quality of whatever people find to be good. Goodness, as it appears in goods, is a value only when the name is employed to persuade people to follow particular systems of behavior and to feel in certain ways.

"Goodness," in other words, becomes a progenitor of revenge against its own indifference when it is translated in definitive terms, as though it itself were like a code of behavior, as though it itself were a different kind of being from, say, evil, as though it itself were like a self and not simply a name that can help to clarify who "we" are, who "they" are, and the ways in which we and they are indifferently different.

When we tell stories and engage in thinking without revenge, options to orders in the name of goodness can emerge. One such option occurs when people translate affirmatively the indifference of time. That option presents a different disposition for commitments and beliefs. Whether self-overcoming or translation comes to the fore of our recognitions, orders of transformative expectation emerge; the heavy-handed seriousness that often characterizes Western morality and universalization decreases. Another kind of entertainment of options and differences emerges with an altered type of concerned energy—not so much beyond good and evil as different from the polarization and its ordering force. It is an issue of sensibilities, of cultural dispositions that people seldom recognize. It is one of attitudes and options that come into view with discursive influence and form knowledge and practices outside the sanction of goodness's name.

EIGHT

Indifferent Love

I turn now to consider certain of Friedrich Schelling's thoughts on love. He developed one of the most persistent notions of indifference in our philosophical tradition, and his thought picks up especially a Pythagorean strain that is embedded in the Platonic lineage. In that lineage Pythagorean images and hopes have exercised considerable power in the formation of some aspects of European and American spirituality. I have chosen Schelling because he knew that indifference is a pervasive aspect of differentiation, and he learned by severe experience that it defies the best systematic impulses in Western metaphysics. In fact, for Schelling indifference and love find their numbing coherence in their differentiation, in what he called their purity and what I prefer to call their freedom.

Schelling's thought, he says, is "an image of inner spirit" that emerged out of his body. When taken on his terms, his thought composes a "circulation between the corporeal and the spiritual," a transfiguring process that is moved by his soul's love for what is highest in its own powers and moved as well by a profound compassion for the corporeality that undergoes the transformation (62, 248).[1] His thinking carries out a process of liberation, ages old, a process that all of nature lusts after and resists, a process that liberates lust in a transformation into love; his thought embodies the corpo-

This chapter is a reading of selected parts of the 1815 version of Schelling's *The Ages of the World*. I will not attempt a comprehensive summary of this work or a comparative study of its ideas in relation to other texts. I find that Schelling's thought, as I engage it, requires that I differentiate myself as a thinker from it, and this discussion comprises a work of such differentiation as I encounter his thoughts on indifference in this fragmented and forceful essay on God's life.

1. I will give the page numbers for citations in the text. The first number will reference Schelling's The *Ages of the World*, trans. Jason M. Wirth (Albany: State University of New York Press, 2000). The second page number references *Schellings sämtliche Werke*, ed. K. F. A. Schelling (Stuttgart-Augsburg: J. G. Cotta, 1856–61).

real sacrifices that figure the soul's rising to its spiritual destiny. As Schelling thinks with systematic discipline, he, in the imagery of his thinking, begins to fade out. God's self-enactment is given disclosive space. The dynamic system composes the soul's movement and thus God's movement, composes a power of life that means the unity of everything. This thought in its discipline moves with an indifference of love that, like a shock of unexpected ecstasy, takes people from themselves, in a sense diminishes them to insignificance, and brings them with alertness to a region of life where their souls, in the soul's vast difference from a particular individual, feel at home, articulately at home, creatively and expressly at home: In his system's movement, Schelling comes before a vast difference from himself. If he can serve the soul well, his system of thought will say what is true, say the truth even in the particular system's failure, like just persons are able to show justice even in their injustices and in their suffering injustice. Schelling will show himself to have failed, but the system's expression will have shown the ground of his failure, will have given him cause to celebrate a cloudy presentation of an unimaginable purity of connections, unified by necessity's freedom and defined by indifferent love.

I would like to consider Schelling's conceptual image of love-with-indifference. If my preceding observations are accurate, this image of indifferent love will not only figure the soul's love. It will also figure the transformed desire (above I said lust) of nature and the faceless, incomprehensible indifference not only of the soul's joining force but also of pure divinity beyond God, "a devouring force of purity," a force of simple and thoroughgoing neutrality, equi-valence. In its imagery and particular difference, his thought, of course, will fail. His articles, "a" and "the," will suggest determinate difference where he knows there is none, for example. And the particular corporeality and specific organizing power of his articulation will make impossible a full expression of his soul's movement and of the ungrounding ground of this movement. But his failure might also give flashes of intuition. It might intensify alertness in the intuition that saturates his thinking as his thinking struggles to be a fully liberated, ensouled act of being. And such failure might also show love that in its indifference exists however vaguely throughout Schelling's thought—throughout his soul's life—as he understood it.

As I work on Schelling's articulate sense of indifferent love, I believe that I am working on a tortured articulation of an image, usually tacit, in our lineage, one that certainly precedes Pythagoras, and one that dimly figures images of divine transcendence. It is an image and sense that traditional Judeo/Christian thought has struggled to overturn by means of aporetic, finite disclosures of divine and personalized care. Schelling's thought is saturated with both pre-Judeo/Christian and Judeo/Christian sensibility and imagery regarding divinity. Its virtue is found in its uncompromising effort to hold together the tensions of his terribly complex religious heritage. Perhaps Schelling's thought gives another birth to an awful body of misshaped images. In any case, he gives expression with little compromise to some of the deepest strands of contradiction and hope in our tradition and in the process brings to determination the kind of reflective obsession that comes from riddles, on the resolution of which our lives seem to depend.

Schelling's complex concept of indifference also holds our attention. It is a formulation that is filled by quite specific images and experiential references as well as by sizable leaps of speculation. His sense of indifference has one of its culminations in its combination with the meaning of love. Love is a word, of course, that often suggests, in contrast to "indifference," intense and personal engagement, a unique combination of affirmation, understanding, dedication, and differentiated effect. Loving appears to particularize both the loved one and the one who loves. To love would seem to mean to differentiate. There are, on the other hand, in our lineage, experiences of a generalized love that constitutes a forceful predisposition, a state of mind that means a pervasive change of character from one that is self-seeking, hateful, or careless to one that is already life-affirming when something particular chances to happen. We know from many venerable sources that if we thoroughly love and attend to what is highest and good we will be in a position to become obedient to it, if not perfectly, at least by intention. We will be inclined to carry out with the required discipline and sternness our love of what is highest and best, and loving differentiation will occur as we attend to this discipline regarding whatever we encounter. Then our lives will compose a testimony to what is most worthy of love, even in the sorrow or guilt of our recognized failures. In such lineages people know of a strange indifference that happens with loving: It is an indifference of love already in act when anything in particular happens.

Is love in an indifferent or in a personal sense characteristic of what is most worthy of love, the force and ground of life? Schelling will answer that it is indifferent love that characterizes the ground of life, and that claim accompanies a narrative of the forces of life, a narrative that might be described as addressing a movement toward a promised land or addressing God's gift of redemption. Schelling's narrative could also be described as addressing human creativity or the purposes of nature. We can describe correctly in several ways Schelling's narrative. In any case the theological content will hold much less interest for us than his way of addressing a dimension of indifference in what is most divine as well as in what is most important for people. Schelling's sense of indifference and the perceptions of this sense will define the limits of this chapter. That sense will be most defined when he speaks of love. We will see that "love," far from the circumscription of persons, can carry utterly nonpersonal meaning and that the meaning of "love" is entwined with senses of neutrality and lack of concern. The interplay of indifference and differentiation will especially draw our attention as we consider Schelling's thought in *Ages of the World*.

THE SOUL

Schelling says that our knowledge of the past is properly articulated as narration. As he re-presents the soul's history—as he tells that story—the soul is presently active and presents itself in its own discernment (xxxv, 199). This combination of knowledge of the soul's past and immediate discernment means for Schelling not only that the soul composes an agency that far exceeds in reach and composition a person's identifying personality. It means also that the soul's present discernment of itself is indispensable in constituting a knowledge of its past. It can tell its own story on the basis of self-remembrance and self-recognition as it engages past narratives, images, and thought. The life of the soul is primordial and ancient beyond days, although it is also subject to unfolding and, by its inherent standards, to present and future maturation. The issue facing Schelling is that of the soul's self-recognition, and, in that recognition, its rising to its highest and ongoing self-expression. The medium of self-recognition that Schelling carries out in *Ages of the World* is that of thinking. The purpose of that kind of soulish activity is self-knowledge in self-reflection. As Schelling thinks systematically he understands himself to think in the very logos of the soul: He understands himself to think in the primordial interconnectivity of the powers of the soul and to find the soul present—to find it existing manifestly in the life of his thinking.

That means that Schelling's thinking moves with the powers of all of life. It means that, as a power of life, his thinking is not so much *his* thinking as it is his soul's coming into its own age and, perhaps, reaching its majority, reaching it freely, out of itself, purely, with a will that is solely its own—the soul's own reflective free willing after so long in nonreflective bondage.

The short version of the soul's connection with persons is that it provides an opening, just like the Pythagoreans and many ancient seers said, to what is outside and above the world (xxxv, 199). In this connection gifted and disciplined people can see the beginning of the ages and, had Schelling finished his trilogy, presumably see also the end and accomplishment of the ages, no matter the fragility of such accomplishments. The soul enjoins individuals with the basic work of creation, with the originary and ongoing dynamics of life. In fact, the soul's accomplishments in the instance of some creative individuals and its accomplishment of free self-realization in them have a ringing cosmic effect as a pervasive and divine work, giving the mountains and the hills reason, as Isaiah says, to break forth into singing and all the trees of the field to clap their hands (Isaiah 55:12).

The soul's accomplishment in its freedom, however, happens as a striving, as an ongoing willing. Its knowledge and emergence from itself to itself can be known only as a work in progress, can be known only in continuous engagement, confrontation, and internalization of whatever is met, whether it be an ancient fable or a natural, scientific discovery. The goal is spiritual unification of all knowledge, experience, and indeed all beings. We are speaking here of soul-making as a process that arises from the soul and is entirely specific to it as people live in their external environments and make those environments their own. In the soul's maturation its work is never done. It's an open future for creations of all kinds because the soul's free life is filled with incompletion and futurity. Its purity is not perfect and is never fully actualized because, in part as we shall see, of its indifference.[2]

POTENCIES

The soul's life is a microcosm of the whole of life. When Schelling thinks of God in *Ages of the World,* for example, his thought is, on his terms, within the soul's space and jurisdiction. The history of spiritual life takes place in this space and plays out in any soulish activity. If Schelling's reflections, as I noted, have the fortitude and discipline to remain true to their soulish life, they will move in their reflective, systematic necessity in accord with the soul's primary movements; his reflections will have their dynamic being in the very heart of the soul. They will then compose a reflective life that mirrors all phases and conflicts among the originary capacities of life, and this mirroring will happen strangely and inversely.[3] It will bring life with its tempestuous and unfree conflicts to spiritual expression and unity. So when

2. Schelling puts the point nicely when he says, "Human beings keep rejuvenating themselves and become newly blissful through the feeling of the unity of their being." Such feeling, however, is supplemental to the need for continuous reflection that specifically carries forth the work of bringing unity to effect in expressions of the natural and everyday world. "[E]verything must be brought to actual reflection in which it could reach the highest presentation" and that by "gradual progress." In a phrase, vision must become historical by hard, reflective, and ongoing work if the soul is to achieve its goal of giving unity and spiritual life to all things (xxviii–xxix). We shall see that freedom, far from a caring way of being, is indifference that makes all the difference in the life of the soul.

3. The inversion is profoundly soulish according to Schelling. It is in accord with the soul's "circulation" (*Umtrieb,* which Wirth translates as "annular drive"), its movement that turns away from and toward itself, perhaps something like a Möbius strip where inversion appears as intrinsic in its infinite, progressive return to a given point.

Schelling speaks of the potencies, of natural and divine contestation, of necessity and freedom, of God, or of divinity as such (*Gottheit*), he is addressing at once the soul's life.

In this address he also intends to enact and stir—to stimulate and lead toward—the highest spiritual life. The soul, as I noted, is not an accomplished entity in Schelling's thought. It is never all here. In its history and in its nascent state, the soul is an interactive, seething process of assertions, negations, and refusals by contesting powers. Absences in the soul, such as those figured by not-being-here-now or by not-at-all-the-other—such absences are alive, weirdly effective, certainly affective. And the regions between differences are dynamically alive. Although the soul is not all here, it is *pervasively* alive, suffering the insufficiencies that move it, longing wildly for missing freedom, undergoing blind urges toward destruction, and envisioning, usually inchoately, strange promises and enticements to something it cannot grasp or figure, promises and enticements that are somehow from itself and to itself and that draw it out and toward what feels like death. Such confounded, living concurrences happen in the past of reflective life and offer a dumbfounded, nonreflective present basis for reflection, offer such captivity for release by careful and disciplined thinking. Such thinking answers from the soul, autonomously and redemptively, the enslaved aspect of the soul's life. As Schelling spins his tale of the soul, if he spins it well, he will fade out, and the attentive hearer will find a soul's nonreflective longing opening out to sympathetic and reflective envisagement, will discover, perhaps, what spiritual suffering *is,* will undergo most likely profound dissatisfaction and sorrow, and will at least feel what the soul's happiness would be like were it to take place. All of this by means of verbal, reflective, and imagistic circulations that mirror each other, interweave with each other, forming a dynamic and thinking space of soul that feels, sees, engenders, and passes. And, as I will say with detail in a moment, that knows of the indifference of love as this living space of soul comes reflectively into its own.

When Schelling uses the word *Potenz* he has in mind living potency, forces of natural life, of God's life, and hence of the soul's life. The potencies are forces of interconnection, withdrawal, and coming out. They define manifest and actual beings, and they bring into effect gaps of life within life—those strange intervals that neither allow nor dissolve palpable connections. They can potentiate living nonactualities such as those of absent and nonmanifest beings, disconnections, refusals to appear, or abilities of being that has not happened. The meaning of potency in Schelling's thought reflects soulish, temporal, and palpable experiences as well as cosmological events. "Potencies" refer to ways life happens when life's happenings take place in a movement of reflective spirituality. They are key players in Schelling's thoughtful story of the soul's development, and, of course, they are key players in the life of Schelling's thought.

The first potency comprises negative restriction of being when God withdraws into itself and in that withdrawal is not manifest. Schelling calls this ontological restriction an empowering "negation" and describes it as concealing (15, 223). A deathless aspect of being is not manifest in the whole entirety of its eternity, and, not wholly manifest, it is never an actualized and present entity. This first potency means an in-itselfness of being, its seeming preservation of itself, its vast excess to any manifest actualization. Schelling speaks of it as a beginning, as always other to a manifest identity. We might refer to it as the always beginning whole. Hence Schelling's description of it as the *first* potency, the one with which any spiritual ascending begins and the one to which any full circulation of being returns.[4] It is the power of no-revelation at all, the perennial Hadonic mystery of sheer absence of light and presence, the closest and farthest vis-à-vis light that never ends.

Schelling also describes the first potency by reference to will: "Each being primarily wants itself." Such urge and its circulating force are without identity but compose the dark and unreachable basis for striving for manifest identity. This first potency suggests for Schelling not-a-being looking to be something. It is sheer wanting without being what it wants—a powerful, an overwhelmingly powerful urge as indeterminate darkness that disallows specificity. The first potency belongs to spiritual light as its primordial, eternal, but longing negation.

In the first potency Schelling finds in living events an eternal withdrawal from life insofar as "life" means at once something that is present and manifest. In his specific language: "[W]hat is altogether the first in God, in the living God, the eternal beginning of itself in itself, is that God restricts itself, denies itself, withdraws its essence [its *Wesen,* its living being] from the outside and retreats into itself" (17, 225). This beginning of life is always happening. That is, this hunger, this vast, starving, blind urge to be something is always happening and composes a dark hole in the originary middle of spiritual life. Were this rapacious need ever to cease, there would be nothing. It is absolutely necessary and without freedom.

The second definitive potency of life that Schelling identifies is "infinitely self-granting and self-communicating" (17, 225–26). The insistent

---

4. "That original necessary and abiding life hence ascends from the lowest to the highest. Yet when it has arrived at the highest, it retreats immediately back to the beginning in order to ascend from it. Here we first attain the consummate concept of that first nature . . . , namely that it is a life that eternally circulates within itself, a kind of circle because the lowest always runs into the highest, and the highest again into the lowest" (19–20).

refusal of being—the first potency—insists on its own happening of withdrawal, constitutes a daemonic affirmation *in* its hunger of its hunger, as though indeterminate hatred-in-hating constitutes a frightful affirmation. There is no sublimation of negativity in positivity. There is simply abiding difference as affirmation emerges from the mad compression of refusal in itself. The first potency also begets its own actuality, the actuality of its own refusal. The second power begins in the affirmation of negation, like an alien that takes refusal of manifest being and makes it manifest. This second potency is the staggering force of turning not-a-being into a being by differentiation. Not by destruction—refusal remains, and remains as separate in spite of refusing to connect. It remains so by the turning force of another aspect that is necessary in the movement of blind necessity itself: the necessity of transcending necessity. A "primordial antithesis" happens that means both the bondage of necessity and option to that bondage (18, 227). In this antithesis we find also the primordial scission that makes the strange requirement of freedom and the paradox that enables and plagues Schelling's thought: the paradox that freedom is necessary in life and that free life requires a circulation of necessary hostility to free life.

"The completely reciprocal exclusion" of the two powers composes a connection, a turning and transposing connection, that is, the movement of life: What was contracting and inhibited becomes manifest and outreaching; and conversely, what is present and shining becomes inward and self-negated. And their turning is all at once, not like a line of points but like the happening of an eternal whole. All of nature in this contestation seems to wait for a unifying act—a spiritual act—in which this belligerent connectedness finds a new quality of unity, a new life.

The third potency is a force outside of the primordial antithesis. It is, Schelling says, "the purest potency, indifferent to both [the first and second powers], free from both" (19, 228). It is the power of unity for the first two, their "eternal end" that defines a force of movement in their turning concatenation. This indifferent purity, however, cannot rule the turning by causing it and hence life to cease. It is a separate, constitutive power in life's eventuation that requires what it frees and that does not cancel the other powers in a higher and stabilizing unity. Withdrawal of being and manifestation of being continue, and finding their end in the potentiation of the third is an event that already is turning into the eternal darkness of beginning and to ontic manifestation as well as toward possible spiritual accomplishment: "When [the highest power] has arrived at the highest, it retreats immediately back to the beginning in order again to ascend from it . . . life eternally circulates within itself" (19–20, 229).

We find in Schelling's thought of eternal circulation the imagery of life's movement as a totally indifferent "unremitting wheel" (20, 229). Each power happens reciprocally with indifferent necessity, indifferent manifestation, and indifferent movement toward indifferent unification. Wherever Schelling uses words like eternal, incessant, always, equivalence, pulses of power, negation, and manifestation, he suggests indifference. Indifference in what senses? Indifference in connection with what or whom?

INDIFFERENCE

The senses of indifference that are generally operative in this discussion are those of equivalence, neutrality (or unbiased disposition), unconcern, lack of differentiation (indetermination), detachment. With this word and its senses we are addressing an aspect of the way things appear. In Schelling's language and thought we are addressing the happening of life itself, of God's and the soul's occurrence. I am not presently speaking of people's reflective attitudes, as when they do not care whether some other people are needy, or are indifferent regarding the possibility of rain. I am talking about the happenings of lives, of our lives and the lives of things around us. The question is whether there is an aspect or dimension of living occurrences that happens indifferently such that our caring, for example, happens with a dimension of indifference—or our judging, choosing, and loving happen indifferently in their differentiations. If "indifference" does determine the way living events take place, how might we understand this dimension? What difference might the manifestness of indifference make?

Schelling's thought in part 1 of *Ages of the World* requires us to see that everything that is differentiated comes together indifferently in the sense that, like gravity, the force of gathering, the absolute power of the whole, brings whatever comes to be into conjunction, brings conjunction with complete detachment before particular interests, intentions, or needs. Schelling's thought is not only a narrative saying *that* the occurrence of potency is without care, is faceless, is without mandate other than its own happening. The thought of indifference is both an intuitive and systematic happening that is itself, in its gathering power, quite neutral, quite without moral or personal charge. This thought is immediately a disinterested force that gives differentiation in the systematic whole. It is the happening of the system without bias or concern for the parts that eventuate in its gathering power.

Schelling valorizes conjunctive, irreducible differences in their equivalence in his image of unity. The co-occurrence of the three potencies, for example, maintains those differences and does not sublimate them in a higher identity. His valorization of difference in the context of equivalence means that even in spiritual transformations of the seething dynamics of life in the raw, the detached neutrality of the potencies continues. No single, ordering power rules the joining of differences. Everything that is differentiated comes together indifferently regardless of the intentions and directions of the participants in the gathering; and this neutrality of joining characterizes Schelling's systematic thought (when it is at its best on its own terms) no less than it characterizes the whole of reality.

A further characteristic of "indifference" emerges: the absence of subjective transcendence in the occurrence of potencies. For Schelling, "indifference" indicates neither a subject nor an object. It applies, rather, to the happening—the *immediate* happening—of something. The immediate happening of an instance of human subjectivity, for example, is not solely subjective. The power of transcendence that is appropriately suggested by the term *human subjectivity* is immediately itself in expression and immediately withdraws from its self-expression, according to Schelling's account of the first two potencies. And the joining of these two potencies in an action of human subjectivity—the indifferent power of their proximity—also immediately happens. None of these powers in its happening is under the jurisdiction of subjectivity or its particular transcendence. None of the potencies is a subject, and each of them is no more nor less than its own immediate occurrence-in-connection-with-the-other-two. So when I know this thing as a hat with all of the factors that come into play in such a personal and objective recognition, there is at once a withdrawal from the occurrence's manifest existence, an out-reaching manifestation, and a force of conjoining unity. Each is qualified by the other two, not concerned with hats, recognitions, me, subjectivity, or the specific meanings of the event. There is in this event of recognition a dark hole, as it were, of no recognition, no meaning; there is also a rush for meaning, and a hunger for spiritualization, regardless of what is spiritualized; and there is the blank force of unity in eventuation. My recognition of the hat does not eliminate or diminish the forces of indifference that happen immediately in my differential recognition.

The powers circulate. The ground grounds. An I happens. The un-ground un-grounds. My recognition comes to pass. All at once. As though for ever.

In the midst of this "unremitting wheel" of beginning and ending, however, there is also, as we have seen, a movement from nonmanifest to manifest (as well as the reverse), a pervasive, if blind, desire for consciousness, and an outward movement that gives up (Schelling says "sacrifices") determinate present existence and gives over to an other (20–22, 230–33). This "redemptive" aspect of life's circulation is like a potency's giving way to what it is not, in part because it immediately desires to be its own event and in part because it has to give over to an other to be itself. Only as an indeterminate space opens up between potencies can the potencies happen as they are, and this movement of giving way and opening space "metamorphoses into a relationship of free belonging together" (22, 233).

On the one hand Schelling shows that even life in the raw is character-ized by an urge for transformation, by a primitive interest in a vague higher way of being. This urge seems to be located in the natural, dialectical inter-play of basic powers as the forces of differentiation interact within the force of unity. The force of unity, in its indifferent conjunctivity, and in its inter-play with the timeless potencies, seems to occasion a desire for unification, a desire that can be met only by means of giving way to differences. Even a state of abject selfishness, a living mirror of the first potency, must yield to what it isn't in order to be its own differential, in order to be itself. That is required by the very movement of life. The third potency, that of indiffer-ent unity, by its immediate force that is only itself and nothing other, does not *intend* that differences seek unity. It is sheer immediacy without a shred of reflection or self-transcendence. But its happening happens as occasion-ing a force toward unity in powers of differentiation. Nothing personal here. But it does mean, nonetheless, a requirement for freedom that can be met only by a sacrifice of the space of an existent's life.

Schelling does not call this requirement for freedom a potency. It—the requirement—however, appears to compose an enablement in life's circula-tion for the transformative force of spiritual creation. This is a force of be-ginning that happens in a voluntary withdrawal of the power of one's exis-tence, a willing affirmation of subjunction to the common of everything, *Seyn*. The opposite of this kind of occurrence is blind obsession and crav-ing that characterize the desire of life that is without conscious spirituality. Voluntary disowning of the force of one's particular existence mirrors the necessity in life of giving way to differences in order to be a specific existent. But the free act is in an order of power different from life in the raw. It is an act that brings mere relatedness to consciousness, to an intended and dif-ferential renunciation. The free act alone can allow that unity the desire for which happens in the indifferent force of the third power.

The move to freedom arises from a scission, a cut (*Scheidung*) between the lives of irresistible drives (in their interconnections). There is an oblique indication of something utterly different from blind nature (23, 233). It's the scission—the occurrence of radical difference—that allows freedom to occur and that sets apart at the same time the region of compelled and un-conscious life. The indicated "Other" is pure divinity, and the scission of complete difference gives essence to spiritual freedom.

METAMORPHOSIS

One of the reasons why Schelling must narrate the past is that narration is an instance of spiritual creativity, as thinking is. The past that he narrates and recognizes is composed of life that desires but has not undergone spiritual transformation (23, 233); it is a past of corporeal life without "sacri-fices" and without a developed capacity to address itself, much less to tell its own story. This past is alive in Schelling's thought and narrative, although up to now it has been unknown by means of activity founded in a scission between raw life and an Other vis-à-vis unfree life. He understands his nar-rative and thinking to include this scission and to compose a creative trans-formation of the raw life of its own spiritual event. Schelling's narrative thought in part 1 of *Ages of the World* composes the spiritual metamorpho-sis of its own active and bondaged life. The multiplied indifference of the forces of raw life continues in the forces' inevitable circulation in Schelling's narrative and thought, and the indifference of the scission and the indiffer-ence of divinity's difference vis-à-vis nature continue. But a kind of Life other to corporeality nonetheless eventuates. This Other is at once "the high-est *concept* of divinity" and spirit without nature (23, 234, emphasis added).

"Spirit without nature" appears to mean that spirit functions completely outside of raw life. Schelling says that the Other, that is, spirit without na-ture, cannot be posited as a natural force. It is "outside and above all po-tency, a lack of potency in itself." It is "without obsession and nature." The Other is not necessarily actual, and "it is not something that is not actual." It is not a being. "It is exclusively the eternal freedom to be." As such it is "above all being" (23, 234).

Schelling also says that people can feel *that* true freedom dwells above being and that such *freedom* can be felt (23, 234). Pure divinity is pure free-dom, and apparently both "it" (as it were) and its requirement for the per-fection of life are subject to affective perception. But, of course, language in this context compels distortion and misunderstanding. Pure freedom is not really anything according to Schelling, not even nothingness. An en-tirely different manner of articulation is needed. Schelling did not have the language or art that he needed, and I think he knew it. But one thing is clear in the context of this discussion: Other than being—pure freedom— is so utterly indifferent that even the existential predicate "is" is unfitting for Other than being. Pure freedom in its scission from existence would be pure indifference were it to be. And were we to say that pure freedom and the in-finitive "to be" enjoy a certain compatibility in their resistance to specifica-tion, we would still recognize that neither "pure freedom" nor "to be" sug-gests partisan or moral qualities. We would see that both terms mean complete indetermination.

In the statements that I quoted, Schelling says as well that the soul has a completely unnatural and uncompelled affection—a soul-feeling—that arises with its own unnatural dimension, with its own dimension of pure freedom. In this dimension, without desire, a "will" occurs "for which all things are equal, [one that] is therefore moved by none of them." Such a will is nothing and everything. It is nothing, Schelling says, insofar as it neither desires to become actual itself nor wants any kind of actuality (24, 235). Pure freedom means an indifference that is indifferent even to joining things—quite non-gravitational, not at all a power of jointure. But "it is everything because *only from it as eternal freedom comes all force* and because it has all things under it, rules everything and is ruled by nothing. . . . For the highest recognition in the exterior sense must be one with the highest affirmation in the interior sense" (24, 235, emphasis added).

Pure freedom: "pure equivalence," "the will that wills nothing," absolute indifference, Other from which comes all force: indifference as nonactive, nonpassive source of all power and hence all movement and hence all life: "the highest," pure goodness. Pure divinity: "pure *actus*": pure consciousness: pure being itself. The highest, therefore, is not a being that either the connections of the potencies can be or the soul in its comprehension of life can be. The highest would be that before which a being can exist appropriately only by sacrificing its determinations and giving way to complete indeterminacy. In such a free act of love a new and unnecessary beginning can take place, one that is outside of raw and selfish life, and one that allows "eternal commencing life" in the voluntary relinquishment of specific conscious enactment.

How does Schelling speak of the occasioning of determinations afforded by pure indeterminacy?

Excursus. Before turning to Schelling's words in response to this question, I would like to pause before a sense and a kind of experience that I expect moved him. I address a sensibility that is consistent with a variety of concepts and images in our tradition but that does not require any one set of those concepts and images. I suspect that it arises as a sense that all boundaries are transcended by mere indetermination, that with experienced determinations comes an awareness of nonboundedness, something like senseless space or simply not anything. This intimation can intensify when boundaries are determined with enhanced sharpness and when things stand out with concentrated identity. In such intensity, identities—determinations, definitive things, and occurrences—might seem especially vulnerable, as though they (or we) in their definitive ways of being did not have to be, as though their definitiveness were in question by virtue of no definitive support, as though definite things were bounded by no definiteness at all. This is a sense of indifference to differentiation—carelessness and neutrality—that accompanies definite and self-projective events. A basic alertness to limits appears to embody this intimation of specific determination as alone in the sense that in addition to other limited things nothing determinate seems to limit them.

There are far more responses to this sense, and in it, than I could know. Many of them are characterized by rituals that can appear to seek order or personality in regions of seeming nondetermination. Others attempt to protect or defend themselves against it. Still others experience a release of themselves as boundaries fade into nondetermination. Often the feelings that occur at the borders of determination are especially heightened and valorized. Sometimes there are feelings of profound and relaxed modification as the strain of determined containment seems to relent, a feeling of being freed that Schelling determined by the meaning of sacrifice, that is, the meaning of a voluntary yielding of the interests of self-determination.

In Schelling's instance the primary name for indetermination is freedom, one of the most determined and inspiring words of his time. As we have seen, it carries a heavy load, bearing not only political and ethical weight but also major religious and theological force. By means of "freedom," Schelling maintains his investment in some traditional aspects of God's "meaning" and departs from those aspects, if not the investment, as well. He maintains in the thought of freedom an image of a system of necessary ideas that in its whole enactment is free. And he addresses what I understand to be his primary experience for thought: his intimation—an intimation that is as close to certain knowledge as he can come—of a region of *geistige* indetermination, indetermination that is, as it were, a free necessity for the being of the world and participatory attention to which enables humans to play a constructive role in the world's continuing creation as well as to become a law for themselves. In thinking through this intimation, Schelling, as we have seen, richly rethinks a historically posited division between mind and body—now nature divided from spirit by a freeing scission. I accept Heidegger's critical observation that Schelling, in beginning with conceptualization, overlooked the worldly, factual, and experiential origins of conceptualization, that Schelling's philosophical world is not appropriately connected with practical and historical life.[5] But Schelling's thought nonetheless begins with diversified experiences of intuition, even though he could not appreciate or even recognize the thoroughly historical composition of those intuitions. These intuitions reflect the noted and persistent sensibility in our tradition that arises with a sense of indeterminate transcendence of experienced determinations. This sensibility often is concealed by theoretical and practical determinations of it. My guess is that

---

5. Martin Heidegger, *Schelling's Treatise on the Essence of Human Freedom,* trans. Joan Stambaugh (Athens: Ohio University Press, 1985), 91ff. In Heidegger's *Gesamtausgabe* (Frankfurt am Main: Klosterman, 1976), Band 42.

Schelling's philosophical obsessions were occasioned by theoretical conceal-
ments of mere indetermination, a hiddenness that is intensified by the religious and theological meanings that defined his intelligence, and by his
efforts to determine indetermination by means of those heavily weighted
signifiers and values. The limits of determination appear to define the limits of meaning, but Schelling affirmed religious meaning even in its denial
at the boundaries of specification. I believe that he would have had to begin
with the withdrawal of religious and theological meaning to have carried
out his sense of indifference. That is a withdrawal that he could neither
imagine nor think. The consequence of this limitation on his part was an
image of pure, indifferent love from which all life springs and a sense of religious significance for nothing.

I return now to the question: How does Schelling speak of the occasioning
of determinations that is afforded by pure indeterminacy? And a corollary
question: When people determine themselves in accord with freedom from
identity, what happens, according to Schelling?

"Occasioning determination" by freedom cannot be a dialectical relationship since for Schelling all such relationships are determined. Schelling
describes freedom as pure will (*Wollen*), and "pure" in this context means
outside of all dialectic and hence outside of all existential contexts: In his
language pure freedom, that is, pure will, neither exists nor does not exist
(27, 238–39). Freedom does not do anything and does not care. In fact, in
Schelling's language, pure freedom is so removed that "it" does not even not
do or not care. Pure, living indeterminacy. Pure being. And that purity
composes its draw to all struggling beings that, in their own living, profoundly and unconsciously enact a share of freedom, that is, of being and
wanting to be struggle-free.

Determination arises with the forces of will, and those forces move
eternally from the first potency's concealing, ground-making, away-turning
power and move toward more life with the outward extending and reveal-
ing force of the second potency. A life hungers for more life, for eternal beginning as well as unthreatened eternal rest—to rest in itself, merely and
richly to be: that is the disturbed, inchoate dream in the will of every living
thing. But to be this living thing means to be joined, to give way constantly
in order to be, always stretching forth to be yanked back toward indiscriminate ground, to being again unsatisfied, threatened, on its way nowhere—
a living thing is constantly given up, moved out, negated, and joined. Suffered and suffering, it has no idea what it is for, why it is, or what would
satisfy its will to be. In raw life the potencies require giving way, falling
back, and yielding. Those movements do not make anything sacred, that
is, they are not acts of sacrifice. But they are faint specters of the will's des-

tiny of freedom. They form the dimmest impression of human being's highest act.

That is why Schelling says, "nature is always an abyss of the past" (31, 244): When a soul comes to its destiny of free choice and is able to speak of itself, to know itself in the full range of its potencies, it has gone beyond raw and blind life. The soul is beyond its own blind nature, is, as it were, ahead of it, an accomplishment of nature's future, now achieved in knowing what raw life can never know: itself and its story.

The initiatory movement of will in the three potencies' power produces determinations. The draw of life toward freedom happens in "eternally commencing life." In its continuous commencement, life "wishes to escape from the involuntary movement [of dialectical necessity] and from the distress of pining" (27, 239). This agitated desire arises with commencement as "an immediate relationship" with freedom. By virtue of this immediacy even raw life is characterized, in its connective and initiatory happening, by spirit that is elevated above natural necessity. Freedom alone, Schelling says, is immediate in spirit, in the power of beginning and hence of joining. This is an immediacy that comes into its own when spirit consciously yields its existence to freedom and freedom's complete indifference.

I note the multiple levels of indifference, not only those that accompany each of the potencies and the occurrence of spirit in eternal commencement. Those are the indifferences of natural necessity and are stitched into the tissue of all things, of all determinations. To be something is to be composed and moved by a crosshatch of indifferent powers. In determination there is an inevitability of carelessness and neutrality as well as of self-seeking and directed movement. Further, spirit in its commencement provides complete impartiality with whatever happens. Its joining is disinterested. Even the longing for freedom in spirit is blind and indiscriminate, an urge without purpose. Freedom, for Schelling, is not like a magnet, not like a site that draws. There is no continuity of movement from raw life in its commencements to freedom, no subject that looks for itself. Schelling's is a different conception from that of subjective self-fulfillment. The indifferent whole of life's occurrence . . . here supplying the verb is both crucial and difficult. The whole of life's occurrence, as we know, does not do or not do anything. The whole of life's occurrence is outside of dialectical movement. People, to belong freely with the whole with which they happen, must be loosened from their dialectical life. They must make it sacred by giving it up. Then the immediacy of the indifferent whole of life has an effect. It's an effect that stems from indifference and that makes for Schelling a huge difference in human life. But the effect and its differentiations happen solely by virtue of willing's active life and its sacrifice. The will, in giving up itself, engenders—lets commence—an opening, an utterly indifferent opening, in which the soul might bring about a new creation. To be sure, this new creation will be subject to the enchained circulation of life. But it will have in it, too, the mark of spirit's freedom. It will carry a scar, as it were, in its necessary tissue that marks a scission where freedom happened and allowed its birth. That scar—is it more like a river?—is like a promise that life is not bound to mere repetition. It can begin with newness, and human being, like God, can occasion free creations.

LOVE

The grim, in-drawing and negating first potency is not totally without futurity. Although it is the force of withdrawal, concealing and locking in, when we see it in the context of the soul's complexity, of which it is a necessary part, we can see that it is in a context of longing for liberation. Although in the first potency the soul is closed off, self-protective, and apparently unreachable, in its second potency the soul undergoes unrepressed, manifest continuance in spite of the curbed and subdued aspect. In its third, the soul finds connection with negation and out-going, liberating self-expression. Schelling says that the crotchety old first potency, in its connection with the second potency, gives rise to the possibility of the soul's love. Without the first power the second power could not be, and the soul, in turning to itself (thanks to the first power), feels loving gratitude, drawing the first power into a circle of affirmation (thanks to the third power) in spite of the first power's resistance (33, 246–47). The soul finds itself with a future as the commencement happens. The soul feels itself in the liberation of time. Love arises in the soul as its repression is released in the jointure of the first two potencies. That happening is the soul's happening as love of liberation.

Already, in the power of joining, a scission between necessity and freedom is in effect. The connection of withdrawn life and out-going life by the power of joining effects, however faintly, an imprint of unity, and Schelling says that love arises with this imprint (55, 275). We have an image of becoming that, in an early phase of simple jointure, traces faintly a possible unity of soul. "Love is neither freedom nor compulsion," but the happening—the temporal happening—of the unity of the whole (55, 275). And as dynamic unifications happen in multiple joinings, a sense for oneness, for being without alienation, for life purified of strife happens too. "Love" names this desire for unity that arises with joinings in the third power.

Love also affirms immediately the soul's elevation to perfect being, however distant such elevation might seem, and composes a spur toward new and higher life, toward unity without stress. Blind yearning in life in the raw is transformed into love as the soul undergoes its inward process of unification, first as nature and then as spirit. This process with eternal commencement is one in which the soul comes toward its higher self by means of unifications intrinsic to connecting. It is attracted by the prospect of its own elevation, its own grounding of differences, its own transcendence in the conflicts that define it (56–57, 276–77). As it senses its unity in its crises, the soul awakens to its own life, glories in it, loves all of its elements, and thereby loves itself and potentially everything that is.

"But love," Schelling says, "has nothing to do with particularity." He is speaking of pure love. "Love does not seek its own (*das Ihre*) and therefore it can not [be a living being] with regard to itself. In the same way, a Supreme Being is for itself groundless and borne by nothing. . . . [A]nother force must first make it a ground. An equivalently eternal force of selfhood, of ego (*Egoität*), is required so that the being which is love might exist as its own and might be for itself" (6, 210–11, trans. altered).

The force of ego and selfhood is found in the first potency, the one that the soul, in touch with its unity, loves, knowing that only in the force of selfhood does love become real. But love in its eternity as pure divinity happens in the absence of existence, and love in its finite incarnation finds this divinelike absence in a renunciation of its particularity, of its "ipseity" (6, 92; 211, 323). Love never indicates "something to grasp or possess," it "is always stirring, but never satiated"—it never reaches an accomplished state of being (62, 284).

Love, then, finds its essence in a continuous renunciation of existence. We have seen that such renunciation occasions openings for new beginnings. In the opening effect of love, Schelling finds affirmation of pure divinity, pure equivalence, pure opening, pure being, pure indifference. Love allows, but does not stake itself on, any particular kind of accomplishment. It affirms by releasing. It finds itself by losing itself. In its occurrence it composes a divine intuition that knows nothing in particular and that affirms being as such.

But indifferent love is not without effect or affect. Love is one of the "wondrous transformations by which matter is subjugated in the organic world," like, Schelling says, "eyes that let spirit shine out." It not only happens in Schelling's knowledge. Indifferent love also happens in bodies as an "inner point of transfiguration" that changes matter into "spiritual-corporeal being" (61, 283). It brings health to the organism in a liberating process of spiritual conversion of natural bodies: "The balm of life in which health has its origin," Schelling says. "It is the discernible in what shines through the flesh and the eyes in that undeniably physical outflow whereby the presence of the pure, the healthy, and the delightful are at work on us in a charitably liberating way" (62, 284). "The unspeakable . . . streams forth as grace into transfigured corporeality." "Beauty brings matter before our eyes

. . . in its divine and . . . primordial state" (62, 284). Love draws the concealed spirit in the natural potencies in one's own body as well as in the world more generally. Incarnated in conscious beings, love becomes the active power of spirit that distills force and renders matter into its highest existence.

The image? Pure love pulsates and radiates. In the careless and overwhelming Other—on its outer fringe, Schelling says—spirit-bodies find their own destinies, their own spiritual nature, a microevent of renunciation, now a distilling of matter into its essence, a gentle "softness" that is moved by delicate beauty, subtleties of spirit that the spiritually accomplished see and know and love. Love's transformations conquer brutality, dumbness, and crude insensitivity, not by teachings primarily and not by codes or laws but by the divine and finally irresistible force of love.

I take Schelling to mean in part that his own agitated, troubled, obsessed, and often patronizing writing composes a work of love, gives indifferent spiritual sight that, by the accomplishment of an indifferent system, no matter how imperfect, carries out and figures the divine, losing always, of course, the unbearable and unfigurable, but feeling nonetheless—and saying and thinking—the implacable draw toward the unity of love, so distilled that it does not exist and in not existing yields again and forever commencement, yields pure affirmation of life. A unity of life and death? Yes, without doubt. For Schelling, the soul never stops dying, and only in that immediate knowledge of always dying does the soul find its life, its determination with indetermination. In that sense, the soul's hope happens with the indifference of life-death, and its transformation by love happens always in an immediacy of loss. The soul's love is at once a knowledge that love of loss figures love of life's beginning, that if love has a secret, it is indifference, and if indifference has a secret, it is love. Love, life-death, beyond care, in a work of care, beyond meaning, full of meaning: paradox with obsession—the destiny of indifferent love.

NINE

Trauma's Presentation

The secret source of humor itself is not joy but sorrow.
—Mark Twain, *Puddin'head Wilson's New Calendar*

I would like now to take a small step toward considering a dispositional change consequent to recognition of the dimension of indifference found in daily living. This dimension can find expression as distance in intense presentations of threat or pain—indifferent distance, a powerful absence of personal dimension in events that we experience as thoroughly personal. How might people appropriate traumatic indifference, neither denying it nor capitulating to it, but rather finding a transforming, mimetic manner of living it through?

It's a question of how trauma happens and how it carries on. There's distance to it as it comes presented. It can be presented to us photographically or verbally, more or less dramatically. Often without words or images. It might be presented in pictures or in a twisted smile on the palsied face of a child who was thrown by his mother against a wall when he was two months old—presented in a paralyzed face that shows while smiling a trauma that is past, certainly, and also strangely present. Traumas persist—remain as presented—in symptoms that carry forward the shock, in manners of sorrow and mourning, in phobias, obsessions, self-pity. These are all manners of memory in which a terrible shock or injury is infused into lives later and after the initiating event. It is infused as well by a dimension of detachment and indifference, a dimension that comes with the differentiating forces of what we call trauma. This dimension is the subject of this chapter.

SEEING TRAUMATIC EVENTS FROM AFAR

Susan Sontag writes of "photography's view of devastation and death" in an issue of the *New Yorker* a few years ago ("Looking at War," 9 December

2002). Looking at pictures of corpses, of Vietnamese children screaming, burning, running from their village, doused with napalm, of ribbed children starving—what are we doing? We are at the very least seeing what we believe to be an accurate portrayal of instances of human devastation, seeing, Sontag points out, by means of a recording machine, a camera, that in spite of its inevitable perspectives gives us a sense of objectivity that the art of Goya, for instance, cannot give. Sontag shows that while early photos of disasters were often staged, during the last half-century such counterfeit practices have been largely abandoned. We have an increase of unstaged and untampered presentations in part because of the extraordinary technical capacity of cameras to go where the action is and to record it as it happens, and in part because the near omnipresence of television's immediacy makes photographic forgery very hard to pass unnoticed. A recording device in human hands bears witness to traumatic events with absolute indifference to the scene, while the differentiating effects through the reproductive and defused perspectives of the news media and commentators can carry huge impact and make important differences in attitudes and policies.

In her observations on "the iconography of suffering," Sontag calls attention to that segment in the history of art that presents "hard-to-look-at cruelties from classical antiquity—the pagan myths, even more the Christian stories [that] offer something for every taste. No moral charge attaches to the representation of these cruelties. Just the provocation: can you look at this? There is the satisfaction of being able to look at the image without flinching. There is the pleasure of flinching" (88). Another dimension of indifference emerges: not that of the machine or of simple curiosity, but that of an act of seeing and digesting what is seen. It is an indifference of distance—it's awful but it's not my face being shot away or anyone's in my immediate proximity. I, seeing the picture, am entirely free to look carefully, to see the engraved image of the bursting nose just as it breaks away from the cartilage that formed it and see the red exploding grains begin their trajectory of dissolution through the air. Gosh, I wonder what that instant feels like. This is so terrible! War *is* evil! "The rest of us [we who see the photographs] are voyeurs, whether we like it or not" (89), she says. There is an indifference in the act of perceiving to which a voyeuristic viewing is entirely attuned.

There's an indifference of presentation built into our seeing even when we are also outraged by what we see. It's the availability of trauma for nontraumatic, perceptive experience that I am focusing on at the moment, the availability that defines a space of nontrauma and carries with it simple unconcern for what is experienced. Regardless of our manner of response—horror, Schadenfreude, curiosity, moral outrage—the event comes as a presentation, more or less reliably fashioned in its particulars and frankness, providing a framed and limited objectivity, a report (no matter the manner in which we receive the news). Such presentations of trauma and their perception in books, newspapers, and television are themselves not necessarily traumatic, and they produce a situation of extreme distance from what nonetheless appears with greater immediacy than is otherwise available to most people. Pitiless delectation seems to be an important part of making traumatic horrors come, as it were, to life for those at a distance from them —and, as we shall see, for those who have suffered them.

Would we want it otherwise? Would we want traumas portrayed traumatically? Would we want nonvirtual trauma, *real* trauma in the presentation? Probably not. Better to let trauma be gone. The indifference of this distance seems to have considerable value, a value worth preserving, a value best not moralized and criticized while we benefit from it. It's the value of letting trauma go even in presenting it.

TRAUMA'S BODY

A trauma is not necessarily at first a meaningful event, but it always makes a physical difference. It produces emotions. A trauma is a neurological recording no matter whether it comes in the form of a realization that a previous and relatively painless experience was one of sexual abuse or in the form of an immediate experience of pain and violation. Some traumas do not arise from events that are directly harmful to a body. They can arise from the force of values and meanings that tell us about what happened to us, tell us that because it happened we are not who we think we are, tell us indelibly, perhaps, that we are going to die, that we are terribly vulnerable in our lives, that we have unwittingly done an evil thing, or that we are victims. These are traumas of identity. We can polish them and keep them on display because they arouse sympathy or pay dividends or make us feel important. Or they can provide a painful basis for new discovery, for the formation of new values, for growth in our sense of our selves. Traumas have meaning for good or ill in social worlds and contexts of words, images, truths, and personal histories. But there is also a dimension of traumatic happening that is neither limited nor exhausted by meanings and values.

As we consider this physical dimension, let's assume that we are in a dimensional and complex region, that the dimensions of meaning and those without meaning happen together for most people most of the time. I am not moving toward a conclusion that separates meaning and nonmeaning in human experience and that would say in effect that people have experiences with no meaning at all. But we are able to perceive and describe dimensions of experiences that are without meaning, and the loss of a sense for these dimensions (as well as for a dimension of indifference) is detrimental for our attunement to our lives.

Trauma happens as a somatic disturbance.[1] The regulation of a person's emotional responses and survival behavior (which is located in the cerebral cortex and in the brain's limbic system) is impacted extremely in a traumatic event. A series of instinctual processes take place as a body registers an impact that is felt as life-threatening: The limbic system signals cells to prepare for drastic action; the autonomic nervous system becomes dominant and sends hormonal signals by way of the amygdalae, the hypothalamus, and the adrenal glands to all crucial organs, flooding the bloodstream with special chemicals and hyperactivating neurotransmitters. Respiration and heart rate increase and provide more oxygen for muscles. Blood is sent away from the skin so the muscles will have more of it. The body moves instantly away from homeostasis and prepares to protect itself, whether by a freezing response (tonic immobility) or by increased movement. These are all automatic survival actions with physical lineages that vastly exceed both the stretch and capability of human consideration. We may call this a normal and healthy adaptive survival response. At best it subsides when the impacting danger is past.

This kind of somatic occurrence, however, does more than respond to dangerous immediacies. It produces a prereflective memory trace that can operate as though the past danger were present. The amygdala function apparently knows nothing of place and time and is also a center for instinctive memory. The function of the hypothalamus, on the other hand, provides spatial and temporal context for events. As long as there is cooperation between these two functions a person experiences a traumatic event as past and can remember its emotions in a spatial context as well. It was then at that place. But if there is only amygdalic impression without hypothalamic qualification, the instinctual memory in that dissociation will lack context, and the traumatic stress could come to presence at any time or place. The situation will be as though the traumatic event were not past whenever something triggers this timeless, placeless memory—the thunder might trigger the emotions I had when the bombs were exploding; your loving caress might unleash the terror of being violently hurt. When the amygdala's memory dominates, a person does not have a clear sense of having survived. It's not that one thing reminds a person of another thing. It's that

1. For these remarks on the physiology of trauma I will draw from Babette Rothschild's helpful report and discussion in *The Body Remembers* (New York: W. W. Norton, 2000), especially part 1.

without hypothalamic function, the reminder lacks temporal and spatial identity.[2]

The higher the degree of hypothalamic impairment due to traumatic stress, the lower the degree of control and management a person can exercise in relation to a traumatic experience. And the higher the degree of stress-induced impairment in the left cortical structure, which is largely responsible for speech—the more the terror is speechless—the lower the degree of ability for handling the stress constructively and meaningfully.

Just when we would like to make a productive difference in appropriations of traumatic events, we find a troublesome fate: When brains and systems of nerves are damaged by too much stress, individuals have difficulty not only managing the effects of trauma but also making sense of them. In this case the body's faceless functioning comes to the fore; good sense and meaning fade away, and a physical dimension without intelligent, spatial, or temporal intention provides the traumatic presentation of a life. In such situations we are at the mercy of an interconnection of hormonal reactions and may well be closer to reptilian conditioning than to human sensibility. A trauma can be affectively recalled, for example, by a simple increase of heart rate or heavy breathing or the body's posture that is "reminiscent" of a traumatic occurrence.[3] And external triggers for traumatic stress can happen in benign situations by virtue of a color, sight, taste, touch, or smell. These instances of physical memory can be quite independent of what a person knows or wills.

Trauma happens as a physical presentation of danger that is sensed as life-threatening. The somatic aspect of traumatic occurrences is not much different in mice, alligators, and humans. In that presentation the ancient limbic system gains a definitive force. A body responds instinctively in the affects of defense, resistance, and mere urge to be. This dimension of physical presentation carries with it an affective memory that differentiates some sensations by their concurrence with the extreme danger. That differentiation is affected without temporal, spatial, or linguistic context. Limbic

---

2. This atemporal and aspatial memory has a particular importance for understanding the effects of certain kinds of infantile trauma. Rothschild summarizes nicely: "[T]he amygdala is mature at birth and . . . the hippocampus matures later, between the second and third year of life. Understanding the difference in the maturational schedules, as well as the functions of these two structures, provides an explanation for the phenomenon of infantile amnesia—the fact that we usually don't consciously remember our infancy. Infantile experiences are processed through the amygdala on the way to storage in the cortex. Hypothalamic function is not yet available, so the resulting memory of an infantile experience includes emotion and physical sensations without context or sequence. This is the probable explanation for why, in later life, infantile experiences cannot be accessed as what we usually call memories" (Rothschild, *The Body Remembers,* 21).

3. Rothschild, *The Body Remembers,* 36.

awareness is indifferent to such contextualization and specification. It—this dimension of awareness, this presentative force—differentiates sensed and extreme danger, tacitly remembers what its sensations are, and, when the memory traces are activated, triggers the hormonal, neurological chain that constitutes a major part of traumatic experiences. When a traumatized limbic system dominates, we have a degree of stress that overrides other affects, and we have a measure of sensation that is without the affections of reasonable or communal expression. It is affection with no sense of identity. In fact, human trauma seems to have in common a kind of wounding that ranges from shattering a sense of self to putting a sense of self in question. The shattering extremity appears to happen in part because of the uncontrolled magnitude of the event and in part because a sense of self plays hardly any role in the trauma's physical presentation.

Some of those who have undergone intense trauma speak of watching it happen to them as though they were outside of it—safely distanced—and as though they were articulating a vast indifference to themselves in the traumatic occurrence. That occurrence is there—I see it. (Strangely, it's happening to my body but not to me-seeing-it-happen. Who is that man drowning? Looks like me. I believe he's stopped breathing.) But that occurrence is not I. I'm elsewhere.

This distance of I from the trauma's immediacy has its survival value, I assume, in many situations. Or, if not survival, its value in a cerebral release from trauma's power. It allows a distance, in the drowning example, from the feel of the water entering my lungs, the terror of the heart's fluttering, pounding, and slowing, the effects of strangulation. Indeed, the blue of the water and the filtered rays of light, the increasingly slow motion of the body, the stilling of the water where there had been so much thrashing, the white sand rising up to the sinking thing, the light streaming down to darkness—there is something beautiful in the indifference of drowning. But now imagine a dark figure plunging in the water. Something jarring happens. Like a rude awakening. The distance collapses into terrible chest pain, heaving efforts to cough. The affections of vomiting, sucking air, water stinging and congesting air passages, flowing out. Unbearable pressure in my head. Agonizing light. I, having drowned, am now here.

DIFFERENTIATION IN RESPONSE
TO TRAUMATIC EXPERIENCES

I want to note two ways that a dimension of indifference in trauma can continue after the initial event. One is found as people undergo affective disorders in which the stress of the trauma returns in ways that challenge or shatter the self's specific sense of itself. The limbic indifference to place and time that we've noted operates with its primitive memory in stress disorders, often with an extremity of force that makes normal daily living impossible. In these situations indifference appears, not as a distance in presentation but in blind inappropriateness for given circumstances and in a destructive noncoordination with the abilities of social consciousness and self-direction. Something without value one way or another appears—something without character or personality, without clarity of interest, intelligence, or choice. I am noting the mere indifference of an instinct severed from the partiality and interests of complex human awareness and values.

A second way in which a dimension of trauma's indifference appears is found by means of resilience and forgetting. Freud said that repression happens when a person refocuses attention away from unpleasant experiences, images, or thoughts. But whether such refocusing is a bad thing is open to question. When a person is able to focus attention on something in the future and is not dominated by a traumatic experience—when, that is, a person curbs the traumatic disturbance and not so much excludes it actively from consciousness as simply moves on to an orientation that feels constructive—when a person is able to diminish the traumatized limbic force and define herself by other kinds of awareness, I expect that a good thing happens. This ability to forget might well assume a process of effective therapy. It might assume a strong sense of identity or a predisposition to let past events go. Whatever the conditions of renewed resilience that allows us to make good our losses, we can see that traumatic memory doesn't have to make a major difference in our lives.[4] It is there without differentiation, neutral in its disposition, available for a wide variety of differentiating appropriations. It is heedless in its limbic presence.

Traumatic memory might well make differences as it is appropriated in a nontraumatic context (I know that I can drown in a way I did not know before, for example; I might or might not want to swim again).[5] Or we might live without immediate reference to the traumatic experience. I speculate that limbic memory is variable in its persistence, that there are instances in which it is highly persistent and others where it fades or ceases. In any case, an indifferent dimension of trauma is awkwardly apparent as a life

4. I take the phrase "make good our losses" from Vincent Colapietro, "In the Wake of Darwin," in *In Dewey's Wake,* ed. W. J. Gavin (Albany: State University of New York Press, 2003), 215. He also includes this quotation from Adam Phillips: "Life was about what could be done with what was left, with what still happened to be there" (232).

5. This drowning example is not entirely based on my own experience. Although I have had two slightly traumatic experiences in water in which the limbic system and autonomic nervous system took over, I did not drown. I have spoken with one person who did drown and was brought back to life, and I have a secondhand report from a distant relative who spoke of his experience of drowning and recovery.

goes on without it. It is neutral as to value and to any form it might or might not take. It can be forgettable and without consequence in processes of living. Its memory is sometimes expendable. It need not be, and a person does not need to be with it. From a different angle we can say that the speechless, largely shapeless, careless, and impersonal dimension of traumatic experiences is, in its ineffability, rather more reptilian than divine and is distinctly somatic in its uncanniness.

TRAUMATIC EVENTS AND THEIR WAKE

If a traumatic experience is definitively dependent on a speechless and utterly nonreflective physical dimension in our lives, what are we to say of the *events* that break traumatically into our lives? We have come so far as to see that the traumatized, limbic occurrence is not so much a narrative as a moment—often a recurring moment—of blind reaction, and this occurrence plays a major role in presenting traumatic events. The presentation of traumatic events is not at first one of narration. No one is telling a thing. There is simply a normal, blind, and dumb reaction to a threat to a person's life. There are, of course, many stories to be told *about* the event and its presentation. Let's focus for now on the event and its presentation and see if we can continue to develop a narrative about them that brings out a dimension of them that is considerably different from the narrative aspect with its structure and meaning. Let's see if we can continue our narrative by speaking of instances of indifference to narrativity. I would like for a degree of resilience to happen in the process of this continuation—a counterpoint to traumatic stress—in which a breach in narrativity is presented without obsessional attachment to a past and without a sense of trauma attached to the breach in narrativity. This would be a breach that is attuned to the indifference we are addressing and a kind of resilience that happens in the affect of Mark Twain's words, "the secret source of humor itself is not joy but sorrow."

The untimely death of someone I love is not funny. Nor are the deaths of millions of people by murderous regimes. Nor are torture and many other suffering and deathly things, including drowning and abuse of infants. An event that threatens a life happens without humor or tragedy. It might threaten a person's life or an organism's life that is not yet a person, such as an infant. A traumatizing event might threaten the living fabric of a community or a system of belief. Such destructive threats can all constitute traumatic events. In any case, a violently threatening event simply happens, and when it happens it hits or threatens to hit something vital, something that urges to be. We may call that a limbic hit. Whether or not the event is recognized with reflective awareness, something nonreflective is activated.

At this level the threatening event's sensed violence incites a nonverbal intervention in people's worlds of meaning. A body perceives a threat of violence, perhaps by inference, perhaps by a completely unexpected impact. The event that incites, incites by impact, by intrusion, by destabilizing expectations and harmonies, by dissociational disturbance. Part of its wounding force is in the event's refusal of operating rules, its shock value. Of course, an event that is traumatic for me might fit well and with no hint of trauma in another person's or culture's life—trauma is not wed necessarily to any particular context. But when it hits, it hits outside of captivity by whatever is expected as usual and right—and outside of the procedures of control that are necessary for a narrative. The indifference of pastness and distance is needed for that kind of control.

A sympathy between such events and limbic speechlessness seems to take place. Neither one is a story or like a story. Each in its immediacy requires language to remain at a distance. Traumatic events and limbic reaction, in their violence and senselessness, allow that distance, that incomprehensibility, that presence without reason that puts human subjects on edge and sends some of us spinning in obsessional efforts to regain or reflect an impossible proximity to hidden sense. Others react by efforts to invest in traumatic events a patina of hidden divinity or a hope for possible benefit. An event of trauma is as indifferent to human values as the agitated limbic system is. We can turn it virtually by stories and concepts to our values and benefits. But in conceiving a traumatic event we are conceiving something already there and gone, conceptless, violent, speechless, senseless, dangerous. The traumatic event is in its life simply its violent happening, reducible to nothing.

So, fine. That's trauma all right. That's its event. Often there is so much that is lost—parts of bodies, whole bodies, happiness, loved people, locales, societies, innocence, hope, affection, a sense of self. Everything sooner or later. Probably no one escapes being traumatized—it's a tristful story, full of sorrow and punctuated by losses that no words or intentions can capture. And yet, in wanting to be alive, we, in effect, ask for it. We intend to make good our losses. We begin again. We might exaggerate our happiness and confidence and creativity. Sometimes we whistle in the dark and smile when we reach a well-lighted place. We try. Sometimes we exaggerate our losses or cultivate them. We build new systems and write new rules. Unless we are beset by discouragement, and then, if not overwhelmed, we talk. We talk with our friends, our therapists, ourselves. Maybe we look for sympathy. Often, for understanding. We cry and grieve. We drag ourselves through days and nights. We build a new sense of who we are now. We look toward a time when we won't want to quit and will want to find something worthwhile to do. Mostly we want to live well.

I think this aim to live well is part of what Twain had in mind when he said that humor arises from sorrow. I think he knew that he could dwell on his losses, write of them, allow them to control his stories and affections, give the awful speechless a certain mastery of his speech. And he knew, I believe, as he moved on in his life, that there is a diminished future in projects that continually return to past losses. He knew sorrow too well. So he made a different turn. He often said, in effect, "Did I tell you about the billy-goat by the name of Eugene who could never turn down the opportunity presented when someone bent over to pick something up? People said he kept count of how far he had knocked bodies flying and that his aim was to put the heaviest thing around the farm flat over the barnyard fence. Well, one day the farmer's wife, Mrs. Bucklebee, took her basket off the peg on the back porch and went to the barnyard to find the eggs of a setting hen. It was a day that Eugene felt like a challenge to cure his irritability and help his outlook on life. He looked around the corner of the shed where he hung out when it was hot and spied Mrs. Bucklebee coming along humming to herself. He closed one eye, wrinkled the other, and commenced to figure her weight. She . . ." and on Twain would go into his story.

Perhaps that is repression. I think it's probably better called making good his losses, a kind of forgetting that Nietzsche recognized as life-enhancing. It's presenting traumas and sorrow—like the ones Twain lived through—with antiphrasis, with humor and in an absence of big hope—with the intention, as he has Adam say of Sabbaths with Eve in the Garden of Eden, of making it through to Monday.

TEN

The Appearance of Public Memory

At various places throughout this book I have indicated an indifferent aspect in the translation and enactment of lineages in contemporary practices and institutions. I turn to one factor in such translation and enactment: public memory. When we consider public memory by reference to its appearing and not primarily by reference to its contents, we are able to position ourselves to reconsider the meaning of "public." We can rethink the memorial dimensions of what we share in common. Public life happens in appearing events, and without an understanding of appearing and its indifferent aspect we will likely not have a good sense of public *life* or of a nonpublic dimension that is common to it. If the claims of this book are persuasive, that would mean that we would not have a good understanding of a kind of freedom that marks public life, a freedom that lacks determinate content and thus suggests indifferent natality and generation.

In this chapter I shall consider a dimension of public memory that I believe we enact on this occasion of written communication. I am not, however, entirely sure whether to say, "We enact" or "A dimension of public memory that enacts us." Either phrasing has its problems. If I say, "We enact a dimension of public memory," the transitive grammar gives us to appear as agents who carry out and establish by action a dimension of public memory. We who enact seem to stand in some vague way outside of the object of our action, that is, outside of public memory. Can "we" appear independently of public memory in our articulated language, thought, and scholarship? Can we happen publicly, outside of public *memory*? I will answer those questions with a qualified "no" in the course of this chapter.

If I say that a dimension of public memory enacts us, the grammar joins the meaning of subjectivity with memory, that is, it joins us as objects with memory that acts toward us and is independent of our initiatory action. A dimension of public memory would appear to carry us out, to bear us forth, and to establish us publicly. Public memory becomes public in this language in a transitive form of grammatical subjectivity, and "we" appear as an objective "us" in connection with an enactment on the part of public memory. Are "we"—indeed, am "I" as I write and speak these words—an ob-ject of public memory's enactment? That phrasing seems to say too much.

My language in the last two paragraphs has been controlled by the active voice. We or I or public memory does something—acts—and one of these pronouns or nouns receives the action. All the while the language in those statements is making public "us" and the meaning of "public memory" in a voice of activity that manifests a subject that is not the object of its action. If I, for example, do something to public memory called enacting it, public memory happens as an object, and I remain seemingly unaffected by the action.

I expect that we agree that there is something wrong with this way of making "us" and "public memory" public in this way. I expect, too, that you have noticed that "appear" plays an important but understated role in these remarks so far, that I have equated "making public" and "appear," and that I have suggested—or the language has suggested (we're not yet clear about that)—that, as articulate language happens, appearing happens; and in the case at hand, appearing is shaped by an active, as distinct from a passive, voice.

NEITHER SUBJECTIVE
NOR OBJECTIVE

A middle voice that is neither active nor passive is probably not foremost in your thoughts at this point. I will state directly and quickly what I have in mind about grammatical voices, this kind of systematic inflection, in order to set forth a territory of description in which we might make an initial exploration regarding the occurrence of public memory. First, articulate language is best understood as an appearing event that gives things to be public, that is, perceptible and able to be understood in specific and definable ways. Second, appearing events are not primarily active or passive, and they are obscured in their dimension of eventuation if they are described primarily in active and passive voices. Third, middle-voice constructions are usually better for addressing appearing events when we want to consider the way appearing occurs; and since "appearing" and "making public" say almost the same thing, middle-voice constructions are most appropriate when we speak of events of public memory with primary attention, not to the contents of a public memory, but to the ways public memory appears and takes place.

I make these statements in a context of asking about the manners in which making public occurs in our addressing the topic of public memory. I hope to arrive at a point where we can hear the sense of saying that public memory happens in and as appearing, that public memory occurs as an appearing event. If I succeed in this intention, when we wish to understand "public," our attention will be drawn not so much to the content of public memories as to their appearing enactment.

When I say "middle voice" I evoke the grammatical inflection of enactment in which an action reverts to the subject as, for example, in the transitive, middle-voiced statement, "The cook cooks for himself," or in the intransitive, "The window shuts," "The (sleeping) country sleeps," or "Birthing happens." We might also say—awkwardly in our active-passive-controlled manner of speech—appearing appears. In its eventuation appearing is neither a subject nor an object.

In the present context I could say that appearing publicly takes place or happens as articulate language occurs. Appearing publicly is not a subject that does something actively to something else, and language, in being public, does not do something to an object called public. And if I say "public," the word says, among other things, exposed with people and available for their perception. To say "public memory" is to say at once, memory of people, people in memory, memory that is not a private domain or a hidden possession. In the occurrences of public memory, people happen memorially. They appear in an unpossessable, historically dynamic transfer of past events, and the appearing of past events, events that are not themselves present, compose people as people, compose a public world in which and as which people live. So when we say that a public memory happens as this practice or that institution or as these words, we speak in, among other memories, a grammatical memory of a kind of happening that is neither subjective nor objective: The phrase "public memory happens" remembers an appearing eventuation that is not a subject or an object.

This kind of linguistic memory gives us to know that when birth or death or language happens, there need be no subject who does something to something else. Rather, people's lives are eventuating—are taking place —in specific ways; they appear dying, birthing, or languaging.

CULTURAL ENACTMENT

Before saying more about memorial life, I turn to "culture" in order to elaborate a meaning of "public" in the context of memories that are embedded in the occurrence of linguistic establishments.

To speak of culture and memory is to speak of care. Care is a disturbing word. In its history of meaning it suggests loss and grief—it derives from the Old High German word *kara,* which means "lament." Blended into its meaning are experiences of uncertainty, apprehension, and responsibility. "Care" contains a suggestion of anxiety and watchful attention. To have a care is to look out for danger and adversity. To be careful is to be solicitous of things that can suffer damage and loss. To feel care is to feel concern and uncertainty.

Culture and *cultivate* have the sense of tillage, breaking, preparing, and tending ground for planting and growth, for careful nurturance and production. In its broader usage, *culture* means, of course, development and transmission of practices, beliefs, and knowledges. The word also carries in its history the sense of *wheel.* It derives in part from the ancient Greek word *kyklos,* circle, wheel. There is in *culture* an overtone of recurrence, return, and revolving movement. It suggests a defining force of movement on a pivot or axis, a movement in which people are returned to something. Culture, in this suggestion, thus directs us to memory and its power. For when we bring together culture and care, we arrive at a basic meaning that is found in the word *memory,* which connotes return to something vital for people but something that is lost in its earlier and initiatory presence.

This word *memory* has in its history the ancient Greek word *mermeros,* "care for" something losable, from which the Latin *memoria* derives. In its many overtones, the word *memory* suggests mourning, remainder, solicitude, and mentation. The basic meanings of memory in this context are those of presencing with a loss of original presence, continuation with absence of guaranteed continuity, and return to beginnings with absence of a primary origin. When something happens in memory, it is presented in the absence of its original presence.

I have made these philological observations in order to hold in mind from the outset that when we address the topic of public memory we are addressing appearing and cultural memories. In such address, culture and human care are reverting to themselves. I mean that public memory appears as we engage the topic of public memory, and it appears as the care of culture takes place. I also want to remind myself and us together that there is no available, original reality called cultural or public memory toward which we can make our way as though toward a timeless essence. We are culturally and memorially enmeshed immediately. When we speak of cultural memory, there is a return, even a revolution of cultural memories. We are enmeshed in memories that are transmitted nonvoluntarily, quite indifferently, by words in their histories of suggestion.

The word *culture,* for example, signifies (and, I will say, remembers) not only labor that is required for human survival—tilling occurs in the absence of paradisiacal plenty—the word also recalls in its usage the definitive importance for people's survival of a steady repetition of knowledges and behaviors that help them and define them. Culture is like the repetitive movements of a fairly balanced, if somewhat wobbly, wheel, movements that revert to themselves, that is, movements that appear as recall and reversion to certain experiences and meanings that happen only in these appearing movements. And with that memory of the need of constructive repetition, there is another one, the memorial knowledge that practices and values by which we survive must be produced and nurtured; the wheel of repetitive cultural movement finds its shape, dynamics, and beginnings within its own limited figurations, and not outside of its figurations. The word *culture,* then, eventuates as a prevoluntary and prereflective memory of pervasive danger, loss, care, and struggle as well as memory of the value of produced and nurtured continuity and stability. To say that people are cultural means in the word's significance that people survive in occurrences of dynamic and public contexts of memory, that we are formed in memorial processes of return and recurrence, and that together we are living memories of manners of survival in the immanence of disaster. People happen in what I might call the middle voice of public memories, as memories, in appearing, revert to themselves, giving people to live as memorial eventuations.

By holding in mind that I am speaking in cultural memories as I address the topic of public memory, I also intend to bring into proximity a slippage and transformation that appear to accompany memorial events. When, for example, the word *culture* recalls tillage, nurturance, and possible disaster, a person might experience vague, nonvoluntary images of someone's preparing a field or an educational institution or a room in an art gallery. Perhaps not even such vague images, but inchoate feelings occur of rightness and high-mindedness that are accompanied by a sense of distaste for crude and low behavior. "Culture" often brings with it a sense of light and also a sense of something vaguely darker and opposite—a feeling for what is "uncultured." My guess is that such vague feelings and images flicker in some brain processes even in people who are working in as disciplined and objective a manner as possible with the facts that define a cultural situation. Regardless of the feelings and images, it is surely the case that none of us stands outside of the indifferent force of the word *culture* in its significatory life as we consider cultural and public events. That is a force that is carried in the word's use and in its position in a system of rules, inflections, references, and connotations. It is a force of meaning that invests our intelligence and affections, that lives as a part of our brains and composes part of our physical lives. In the enactment of the word *culture,* many nonvoluntary meanings and memories appear and are available for all manner of perceptions. In a phrase, the word *culture* happens culturally.

APPEARING'S MEMORY

In addition to the memories of meanings in "culture," there is also a memorial dimension in occurrences of appearing that does not seem to be dependent on what is appearing. You might recall that I used the phrase "appearing appears" when I described the middle voice. The two descriptive claims that I wish to make are these: The ways in which appearing happens are public—of people—and are thus available for understanding; and the occurrence of appearing happens memorially.

Memorial in what sense?

There is in the occurrence of appearing a vexing aspect that is filled with discomforting implications: In appearing, I have said, something is always at a remove from full presence and possession. I find this aspect vexing because appearances can be so full. There are things that appear solid and stable—floors, earth, well-built structures, thoroughly trusted friends, certain inevitabilities like the sun, moon, and tide. Not to mention such regularities as occurrences of death, lightning, and desire. My point is not that we know that these occurrences could change. I want to note, rather, that in their fullness, appearing things also recede, that an appearance never fully encompasses and exhausts a thing's happening, no matter how stable the thing appears. Appearing gives both presence and loss of presence at once. In an appearance of stability, for example, stability also comes to pass. I will say more in a moment about the memorial aspect of the recession of appearing in the happening of appearing. For now, I note that in appearing, things come forth at a distance—the *appearing* thing is not a complete and finished, fully present thing. Things happen with an elusive and unpossessable quality, even in their full-seeming stability. The lives of things as they appear seem always to elude full encompassment by their appearing. Appearing happens in a recession of complete presence in what appears.

Appearing things happen mutably and transitorily. As far as I can tell, appearing gives what is in appearing to come to pass and to come to pass because it is really, genuinely, unpossessably, palpably appearing. Whatever appears seems to be subject always to alteration. Appearing thus seems to happen with a peculiar memory; its occurrence recalls facelessly the mutability of everything that is manifest, as though appearing were a neutral circle of temporality that wheels whatever appears by an axis of perishability, returning indifferently even the most persistent appearances to the reminders of nonappearing and the need for care.

SUBJUNCTIVE INDETERMINACY

I would like to bring together with the meaning of the word *subjunctive* the recession of appearing in appearing, mutational transitoriness, and memory. I make this move because I want to show that the very happening of public things is memorial—that when we speak of memory we might speak not only of mental events and dynamic institutional formations, but also of memory in the eventuation of appearing itself. And I wish to show that the subjunctive mood is especially fitted for expressing the memorial happening intrinsic to appearing. For as appearing happens publicly, happens with people and their ways of life, a surprising nonfactual aspect also takes place. By giving accounts of appearing we can also give accounts of a memorial dimension in our lives that is not circumscribed by any one group of human practices. This is a dimension of nondetermination in the occurrence of appearing that I am figuring with the words *mutability* and *transitoriness*. It is a dimension of indifferent elision that escapes declarative language and direct, objective engagement.

Although in this discussion I am limiting the field of appearing to words and the memorial histories of significance that they bear, you can see that I am also shaping an approach to public memory that is a grandchild, if not a great-grandchild, of a way of thinking that gives a methodological priority to the dynamics and qualities of appearing. Presently I want to indicate that the subjunctive mood can serve to recall an aspect of appearing that is important when we consider the meaning of "public" and as we think of the memorial aspect of appearing.

I choose subjunctivity as a collecting and integrating word because, in naming a grammatical possibility, it recalls a nondeclaratory dimension of events that is not subject to more literal occurrences—occurrences that are just as we say they are. Or, to put the matter more formally, the subjunctive is a mood of noncompletion contrary to fact. It names a dimension of occurrences that is outside of the range of declarative statements. Subjunctive phrasing indicates or betokens indeterminate contingency, possibility, and mood. So when I said a moment ago that, in appearing, the mutability of everything that is manifest happens as though appearing were a neutral circle of temporality that wheels whatever appears by an axis of perishability, you probably recalled nonvoluntarily that the verb *were* indicated not a fact, but a nonliteral, metaphorical possibility. The subjunctive mood subjoins indeterminacy with a determinate state of affairs and expresses something by reference to an elision, a "gappiness," which is said to be in the way something happens. This grammatical trope integrates by signifying an elision of factual literalness and direction in factual events. The subjunctive mood recalls a nonfactual dimension of facts. Or, I could say, the subjunctive mood is a trope that bespeaks a withdrawal of factuality in the occurrence of facts.

I have named aspects of subjunctivity in appearing: "recession," "mutability," and "transitoriness." And I have pointed out that the subjunctive mood recalls us to an indeterminacy in factual situations. Appearing things —public events—*as appearing,* embody a recall, a continuous return to the very qualities of life that give us to care, to the instability of stabilities, to present things' coming to pass. Appearing carries memory of the necessity of culture, and culture reminds us constantly and publicly that ours is a fragile, appearing world with indeterminacy and mere possibility as well as with factual determinacy. Whatever appears, all public things—axioms, values, meanings, scientific methods, bodies, facts, beliefs, and established practices—in their appearing come to completion in passage and change, and can never be held in a perfection of presence, an exactness of designation, or a language of unfailing engagement. This subjunctive quality of appearing suggests that what is public might be otherwise, is not only factual, and might be found, as it were, in *might* rather than *is.*

RECESSIONAL APPEARING

I will close with some observations on the recession of appearances in appearing and a consideration of the significance of this recession for our accounts of public memory.

In this chapter I have joined recession with the meaning of palpable and suggested that the reality of what happens, the concreteness of experiences and appearing lives, is found in an eventuation that can be expressed by the middle voice and the subjunctive mood. I have said that there is a happy coincidence of this mood of indeterminancy with a voice that is controlled by neither subjectivity nor objectivity. How are we academic disciplinarians to live with that? If the things that we want to understand are, by virtue of appearing and becoming public, forever coming to pass and disappearing, if the very occurrence of the culture that we express and to the life of which we contribute bears witness to the care-filled incompletion of all relations, if appearing comprises a nonfactual determination of all public events, how might we speak knowledgeably of public memories?

I expect that we must take into account the ways in which appearing happens and make that account a definitive part of our scholarly work. If we make, for example, public memory into a quasi-essence by reifying it into something like a historical subjectivity, or if we expect to comprehend appearances as though they were completely present, then the knowledge that we produce would embody a degree of forgetfulness of the mutable and recessive, appearing lives that we address. We will have overlooked a nonfactual dimension of what is public. Such knowledge would forget the *appearing* culture that we bespeak. Our scholarly care will take forms that are not attentive enough to the memory of our culture as it appears. And the structures of objectivity that we in our disciplines intend will miss the voice of eventuation that does justice to the incompletion of whatever is public that we wish to understand.

I think that Foucault, for example, knew that. He continuously, in his broken prose and rambling empiricism, found broken continuities. He found continuities *in* their broken and rambling appearances. He found fragments of unifying disciplines, shards of practices, happily inconclusive matrixes of contradicting values, and instances of cruelty in processes that were also charitable and anguished with good intent. There are many others on the scene who have found in the incompletion of language and appearing things avenues to considerations of lives in their striking appearing and withdrawal from anything that would engulf them with meaning, value, and status: Deleuze, Blanchot, James, Derrida, Heidegger, Dewey, and Nancy, to name a few. One issue upon which they insist places the language of our knowledge at the fore of what appears: Articulate language gives publicity, is intrinsic to what is known and meant, and is filled with nonvoluntary memories that are seldom cohesive and are always forceful. It appears that, in our speaking, we remember much more than we can know as we engage public things in our many ways. This surplus happens indifferently; no one does it. And with this indifferent surplus come the passing incompletions of whatever becomes public.

The question that I wish to underscore is this: How might we care for those vast and conflicting memories in the appearing of things as we speak of public memory? How might we best give voice to the incompletions of those memories and of the things that appear with them as we attempt to make public memory manageable in our disciplines of address?

One way to engage such questions would be to give accounts of the withdrawal of public memories as they appear, to show that *public* no more means full presence than *memory* does, and, perhaps, to show that being public appears to measure a loss of what in an event cannot happen publicly. What might be at stake for a people if publicness drowns out the indifferent quietness of appearing things? Might we measure the cultural import of public memory by reference to an absent presence in its appearing? My guess is that our publicly attending to an indifferent withdrawal of things from the public domain would be important as we care for appearances. Otherwise we might become engulfed by our public truths, our subjective formulations, and our objects of interest. I am suggesting that the life of public memory depends on lives that are never fully public, depends on a recession in publicness from publicness, and depends on losses that can never be restored. In alertness to these aspects of public memory, we might—here's the subjunctive again—find that to speak well of public memory we need to learn how to speak in regard for nothing public at all. As appearing reverts to itself in its occurring, it's as though nonappearing were remembered, as though a public place were not literally a place, and as though we were public nowhere else than in appearing.

ELEVEN

Wal-Mart and the Heavens: The Factor of Indifference

> . . . if eyes were made for seeing,
> then beauty is its own excuse for being.
> —R. W. Emerson

Very early on a February morning I sat outside contemplating the stars, especially Draco and Serpens, Arcturus, Mira, and Spica. The sky was clear, the breeze balmy. Except for the soft rhythms of waves coming to shore, the earth seemed still. I saw two shooting stars. In this moment of reverie I was considerably surprised when, quite involuntarily, a vivid image of a Wal-Mart came to mind. Not Wal-Mart generally, but the specific Wal-Mart in my hometown on Atherton Street. I shop there occasionally and often with reluctance. It is so fluorescently bright, especially early in the morning or late at night when it has the advantages of few customers and a mood approaching leisure. A glare presents the things on the shelves, things arranged not by color and size so much as by functional classifications: clothing, then shoes, then shoes for different purposes: work shoes, children's shoes . . . : things arranged conveniently according to the economies of homes and work, of kitchens, garages, medicine cabinets, entertainment centers, nurseries, decks, and backyards. Things are everywhere, all shelved, displayed, tagged, coded, and ready to be checked out, unpackaged, spread out, assembled, plugged in—used. These arrangements are presented in a glare of light that, combined with the withering number of things (over fifty thousand of them in our Wal-Mart; Super Wal-Marts have seventy thousand different types of things), sometimes leaves me light-headed and on a drift to dizziness. When I go there, I prefer short and highly focused trips.

So why in the world was Wal-Mart a constellation in my mind in this blissful darkness, creating a most singular experience in the middle of my reverie?

Among many possibilities for this association, I emphasize the obvious: antiphrasis, radicality of difference. Never mind the hellfire that is going on in the stars' vicinity. From my vantage point they gave a serenity of light with darkness made all the more drawing for contemplation by calm, warm air and the ocean's rhythmic pounding. Nothing felt especially functional at that time. Nothing glared. Nothing was packaged, especially as I watched and lost all sense of names, without a cart in which to carry picked celestial bodies. Nothing at that time appeared in bondage to human economy: Everything I saw presented itself in considerable excess to the name I applied to it. Indeed, I felt as though part of my sensibility inhabited and was inhabited by a region without name or human dimension. So when the Wal-Mart entered the picture, my fusion with the heavens underwent a marked confusion.

The reclining, plastic, and rustproof chair on which I lay did indeed come from the no-less-glaring environment of a Wal-Mart-like Home Depot. The house to which the chair belonged was largely built and furnished by purchases that were carted to checkout stands, earlier having been loaded by huge cranes into boats' holds that were filled with noxious air, amidst an uproar of people and equipment, before being loaded by forklifts onto pallets and trucks. My dreamy moment was historically and socially conditioned by computers, multiple exchanges of money and labor, the laws of many nations ("Made in China," "Made in Malaysia," "Made in USA"), many complexes of workers, trading companies, wholesale and retail establishments, and individuals (some with retirement and health benefits, some with corporate bonuses, and some with less than a dollar an hour and no individual freedom), all on the earth and under the stars.

On that morning I did not think of these things, or of airports and airplanes and traveling schedules. I simply contemplated, underwent a complex, additional, and unwelcomed sense of Wal-Mart, and saw the quick flash of another shooting star.

Wal-Mart, like McDonald's, has a bad reputation among some people. Its range of selection and low prices destroy small local businesses. Its builders pour millions of pounds of gravel and asphalt over fields that once produced food, provided grazing for farm animals, or simply were open space and sanctuary for plant and animal lives. Its policies cultivate a low-paid, rapid-turnover workforce. It is housed in buildings without beauty or elegance. Its mass-produced goods erase the value of the artisan in favor of the price for styles and goods that are the same in Seminole, Oklahoma, Detroit, Michigan, or Buenos Aires, Argentina. Cheap and functional things replace what is finely turned or hand-sewn. And most of us go into its glare to find the best prices for items that we will discard when they are used up long before we die: I think that most Americans know that it's often much cheaper to go to Wal-Mart and replace something than it is to repair it.

The starry heavens, on the other hand, have enjoyed a good reputation for most of our recorded civilization, figuring as they do senses of nonutilitarian beauty, infinity, mystery, sheer magnitude, something like a magnifying glass on human dimension and finitude. The stars and their elements also mark one of people's most exciting frontiers for knowledge, a frontier where the unknown and perhaps unknowable is present alongside human vision and intelligence. This strange combination of Wal-Mart and contemplated stars forms an experience from which and to which I would like to think for a moment. I believe that this fusion of usual and unusual, of something approximate to ugliness and something else that is so "else" than what we call mundane—such a fusion might clarify a common experience of what is not common at all. I believe that the experience of Wal-Mart appearing in a reverie with the heavens was nonvoluntary, and nonvoluntary not only in the sense that I didn't consciously intend the event. I expect that it was nonvoluntary in the sense that it arose from a situation that I am in and, as I, do not define or create. It arises in a habitation that provoked the con-fusion of resonances that the heavens and Wal-Mart together figure.

First, Sam Walton and Wal-Mart. In order to gain some purchase on the remarkably complex realities that Wal-Mart comprises, I begin with Sam Walton, its founder.[1]

Sam Walton's "philosophy made sense, and you couldn't help but believe in the man."[2] This statement is like those of many others who knew Walton. He was a discerning, personal, self-effacing—he didn't put on airs

---

1. In the following remarks I draw primarily from Sam Walton's autobiography, written with John Huey, *Made in America: My Story* (Westminster, Md.: Bantam, 1993), hereafter *SWA;* Bob Ortega, *In Sam We Trust* (Thousand Oaks, Calif.: Three Rivers Press, 2000), hereafter Ortega; Bill Quinn, *How Wal-Mart Is Destroying America (And the World)* (Berkeley, Calif.: Ten Speed Press, 2000); and Sandra S. Vance and Roy V. Scott, *Wal-Mart: A History of Sam Walton's Retail Phenomenon* (New York: Twayne, 1994). Bob Ortega's book is remarkable in its breadth of reference and the detail of its investigative reporting. Although his book is critical of both Wal-Mart's policies in many instances and the meanings invested in its symbolism, Ortega nonetheless presents—or clearly attempts to present—a fair and accurate account of Wal-Mart, its generative environment, its formation, transformation, and, above all, force as an American phenomenon. His book provides an interesting contrast to Walton's autobiography, which also presents—or attempts to present—an honest and fair account of the author and his creation, the apotheosis of North American retail business. Ortega's book also presents a more thorough and measured account than those books that have as their primary purpose the curtailment or downfall of the Wal-Mart business.

2. This quotation is from Willard Walker, who was the first manager Sam Walton hired and who ran Walton's Five and Dime in Fayetteville, Arkansas, beginning in 1950. He said this shortly after he borrowed money in order to buy stock in Wal-Mart's first public offering. Quoted in *SWA,* 46.

—and vastly energetic man. He liked people. He liked to be among them; he liked to win them over to whatever he was up to; he liked to look into their eyes, call them by their first names, and be in that part of their environment that was secure and friendly. And he loved to sell and compete. His affirmation was infectious. "Hey Charlie," he might call across the street, grinning and waving, "come over here and see this new ice cream machine I've got." He meant, of course, to sell me a cone of his soft ice cream from his new machine that he placed on the sidewalk in 1947 in front of his new Five and Dime in Bentonville, Arkansas. And he knew, as I am imagining him, that he had an innovation in this machine, that people in Bentonville were hot (and also happy about anything new and sweet, and cheap), and doubtlessly that he could sell this ice cream at a small profit and yet cheaper than the drugstore down the block could sell its ice cream cones.

I believe that his friendliness did not come from some unfriendly manipulator hidden in his consciousness behind his persona. Or if it did, Sam didn't know about it. He knew he wasn't reflective, and he didn't care to be. Few "re" words—words that have to do with reversion or going back—would describe his intentions. He was all forward motion: "I have never been one to dwell on reverse. . . . It's not just a corny saying that you can make a positive out of most any negative if you work hard enough."[3] He loved action, moving forward, going out to people, and drawing them in. Whatever served the purposes of retailing had value for him. Whatever contributed to a competitive situation interested him. He loved to be first—to be the president, to be the chairman, to be the center of attention, to win. And in all of this drive he wanted to be one of the folks, to be a part, the winning part, of his community. That's the reason, I believe, that he always kept his phone number listed in the Bentonville phone book (even after *Forbes* listed him as the wealthiest man in the world), had his hair cut in the local barbershop, mostly drove an old pickup (frequently in the company of one of his dogs), visited his stores and employees tirelessly, and spoke of Wal-Mart as though it were a family. He *was* a part of these people—people who had rural and small-town backgrounds and who, if they weren't poor, were close-up and personal with the poverty around them. He didn't have to make an effort to understand them. Like them, he didn't like highfalutin airs, smart-alecky talk, public extravagance (or private either, for that matter), or wishy-washy politicians. He never felt like wasting money. (Money for good bird dogs, fine shotguns, safe tires, a good, practical education for your kids, necessary commodities, and good life insurance doesn't go a-wasting. Money spent on new cars, airplanes,

3. *SWA*, 39.

and trucks might be pushing it unless you drove your vehicle into the ground or got a very high trade-in for a very old car. And money spent on a new filing cabinet when orange crates would do was money lost to a non-necessity.) Sam knew his people, and he liked them with an infectiousness that lasted until his final public appearance when he struggled from his wheelchair to his feet and, though close to death, stood during the long duration of a thunderous ovation from his employees after President Bush (the elder) presented him with the Presidential Medal of Freedom.[4]

I emphasize his down-home, nonreflective sincerity and charm; his competitiveness; his no-frills practicality; his main-street charisma; his utter commitment to hard work; his thorough and disarming acceptance of himself; his sense of decency and fair play; his intelligence, innovation, adaptation, and application; his natural intuition for what common folks wanted and needed—I emphasize these qualities in order to address those very qualities in the entity—Wal-Mart—that he brought into our world. Not just into our world in the United States or in North America or in the American continent, but our world around the globe.

There is something almost offensive—as well as fascinating—in the fact that the largest retailing business in the history of humankind began in Bentonville, Arkansas, by the efforts of a man who liked the town because of its close access to four bird-hunting seasons in the four contiguous states of Arkansas, Oklahoma, Kansas, and Missouri. I think, too, that there is something irritating, especially for people who have yet to cultivate a fondness for popular Arkansas culture, in Wal-Mart's cosmic and definitive impacts, its unparalleled success, and its ability to define retailing for many cultures. It's one thing to note that Wal-Mart could purchase most of the world's available great paintings and rare books as well as finance most of the world's great orchestras—could purchase and support them on its annual budget. But it's another thing to realize that Wal-Mart doesn't give a damn about those things. Or about most other humane matters.

And along with the irritation instilled by the little Arkansas feller who liked to wear baseball caps and who would talk about nothing else than family, hunting, and business is the considerably greater irritation instilled by business practices that are recognized to be as ruthless and careless of major ethical issues—that is, careless of the well-being of large numbers of people—as those found in countless other megabusinesses scattered throughout our history. Such aggravation can explode into rage when people dis-

---

4. "As Bush gave him the medal, the throng of Wal-Mart workers who'd crushed into the room erupted into a roaring, standing ovation that went on for minutes. Walton stood the whole time, waving feebly, clearly proud and touched as he steadied himself with one hand on the wheelchair behind him" (Ortega, 22). He died the next month.

cover, for example, that the rhetoric of "Made in America"—a rhetoric that struck a chord of hope amidst anxiety-filled Americans, including those supportive of the very unions that Wal-Mart so effectively opposed—this rhetoric covered over the retailer's purchase of millions of dollars of goods that were made outside of the United States, that were made in working conditions not much different from those of slavery, that gave Wal-Mart a huge markup, and that on occasion had "Made in America" on their labels.

Who the hell does Sam Walton think he is? Paving our fields, outcompeting all local, national, and international rivals. Talking in his nasal twang about good business practices while all his business cares about is the bottom line.

I believe he is a man who has carried aspects of our culture—*our* culture—to such a point of obviousness that we cannot ignore those aspects. We might disown them, say they're not ours specifically, and blame them on consumerism and automobiles. But this nonreflective man's creation also carries with it an embodied reflection of ordinary people's desires to own conveniences, have access to a variety of clothes, be able to choose among options of goods and times to shop, be unbound from the schedules of mass transportation (which cannot be a whole lot less bland, impersonal, and stereotypical than a Wal-Mart and which can be a lot less sensitive to customer demand than most good retailers are). Wal-Mart's success and approach reflect back to us the fact that in this society, although hard work and discounting are not necessarily keys to success, they nonetheless can pay off big. I wonder occasionally what Sam would have done when he owned his small local store if a huge chain store had moved into his town. I'm reasonably sure that he would have gone to work to find options to beat the SOBs at their own game either there or somewhere else. I don't think that he would have given up or given himself over to resentment.

"That's the thing," as he often said when he wanted to make a point. Resentment and carping and getting into zero-sum games don't get you very far. And that's been true pretty much throughout this society's history. Exploitation of people and resources may help you along toward independence and greater security. Frugality and very hard work can at times make *the* difference for success in business. Although my experience is neither professional nor vast, I have never known a successful businessperson who was not frugal in her or his business dealings, and I have known few highly successful businesspeople who did not appear to be obsessed. Competitive skill, a desire to win, relentlessness, ambition, willingness to cheat when the odds favor nondetection, intelligent cultivation of influences and image, willingness to learn from your opponent, ability in intuitive and affective perception—all these things (which Sam had in abundance) can be great aids to financial and social success in our society. But standing pat, resisting innovation, holding a distaste for mobility, and (unless people have inherited wealth and position) possessing a conservative sense of established tradition have not been special aids for commercial success. Nor have cultivated senses for beauty, ideas, and subtlety of style.

It makes sense that for a long time the majority of Wal-Mart executives did not have a college degree.[5] Wal-Mart was not in the business of responding to refined tastes or sensitive, informed ethical concern. Refinement was not and is not what Wal-Mart means—*except* refinement in such areas as delivery of goods, cost control, computerized business, motivation of personnel, and its huge contribution to the shape our society has taken as it has transformed from a manufacturing to a service-oriented, suburbs-dominated economy. Wal-Mart means bringing an enormity of goods to a very large number of people for the lowest prices in that region. It means market saturation and cutthroat competition. It means appropriation of all methods and approaches in retailing that work toward the goal of selling a huge volume of goods quickly at comparatively low markups. It means easy availability of goods. It means the normalization of part-time work. It means threat to small businesses, small-community ideality, and community tax bases. It means threat as well to other big retailers in England, Germany, France, and Latin America. And, always, it means low prices, low overhead, and low, as distinct to either high or highfalutin, taste. It's a store for the people of its time.

There will probably come a time when folks will be able to buy caviar, excellent wines, top-of-the-line aged cheese, and the freshest available vegetables and fruits at Wal-Mart. And probably top-of-the-line clothes, too. Progress may also put Wal-Marts on mass-transit lines that would certainly be an improvement over Seattle automobile traffic and some present-day subway systems. And perhaps Wal-Marts will begin to buy and restore (at a discount) deteriorating eighteenth- and nineteenth-century buildings in downtown Philadelphia, Florence, or Barcelona to satisfy politically effective critics of box buildings. Or, to the outcry of people who like to live in them, Wal-Mart may buy up blocks of old warehouses on rivers, lakes, and oceans where they will sell for less and people won't have to drive to them. Wal-Mart might well install its own public transportation system and more than likely use tax dollars to do it. If that's what folks want. Because Wal-Mart means what people want and whatever it takes to meet that "want."[6]

5. That was also true for other discount store organizations.
6. There are many instances of communities in which a majority of the citizens did not want a Wal-Mart and successfully rejected the organization's zoning requests. But it continues to grow. It now employs over a million people worldwide and is opening new stores almost weekly.

It's an accident of time and place that Wal-Mart's founder lived in a small town in Arkansas. What Sam found with greater clarity and energy than most other retailers in his time is the object of a pervasive desire in this society—more goods for lower prices—and he began by meeting that desire in the small towns and for the poorly paid people that most large discount businesses overlooked. He loved to meet people's economic desires and carried out his love with more energy and talent—more informed passion—than most other people had.

But the results were not beautiful. They were not even pretty. Sam never said the Wal-Mart buildings and parking lots were pretty. He never said he wasn't a tough (he should have said ruthless) competitor. He learned from K-Mart that populations in cities and towns were shifting out of the downtown areas—downtown deterioration did not begin with Wal-Mart in the 1960s. He utilized and intensified that process. He said that his buildings and parking lots were convenient, and they were cheap. Do you want, he asked in effect, something pretty to buy in, or do you want low prices? Do you want to walk down nostalgia's lane to the pretty little row-store on Main Street with the nice older couple in aprons who run the place—or the picturesque couple who used to think of themselves as hippies? Go to that store that began back in 1872 in a clapboard, later boardwalked version, a store that's been there in one form or another ever since, smell the old smells, have a conversation with the owners about the weather and the last school board meeting, and pay $67 for a pair of pants? Or would you rather drive by Wal-Mart after picking up the kids from soccer practice and buy the same pants from a largish woman at the checkout stand whom you don't know and whom you vaguely imagine has been on welfare and pay $43 for them? Answers will vary, but Sam knew his majority. The thing is, people go to a convenient Wal-Mart for low prices on lots and lots of goods and not for any other reason.

Wal-Mart thus means, unsurprisingly, a broad, cultural priority on economic interests with an emphasis on people on the lower end of the income ladder. Most people cannot afford the cost of things at stores whose overhead is significantly invested in fresh flowers, careful décor, carpeting, lovely ambiance, and other expensive charm factors. And the cost of mom-and-pop operations is usually high—uncompetitively high in comparison with Wal-Mart's—when prorated on an item-by-item basis.

Wal-Mart is blunt, dull, fluorescent, gorged, and surrounded by asphalt. Its retailing practices are usually costly to downtowns. It defeats its competition by convenience, discounting, size, and market saturation (tried-and-true practices in retailing long before Sam). As an organization it is lean and mean, not unlike a pro team playing teams mostly from minor leagues. It grows single-mindedly, reflecting, probably, Sam's own obsession and joyous dedication to "stomping the comp" (competition) by sapping their strengths and hitting their weaknesses, as any well-coached team or large retailer will do. The folks who hang out in Wal-Mart's plastic cafés—largely, as far as I can tell, lonely older men in the mornings and perhaps people who find Wendy's a tad expensive—are not usually among the beautiful people, the social activists, or the intellectually stimulating. Cheapness in cost overrides most aesthetic considerations short of dirtiness or slovenly arranged goods (and in the early Wal-Marts Sam sold a lot of goods that were stacked helter-skelter in buildings that were hardly more than worn-out and unadorned warehouses). We don't necessarily want a good aesthetic experience when we go to buy a bike, underwear, a television, or a watch. The stores are not designed to lift you up or inspire you—if someone experiences reverie in a Wal-Mart, it's not the store's fault.

My interests now are not in ethical considerations except insofar as they have to do with indifference and what I might call prosaically "lifting people's spirits." Lifting people's spirits, not in the sense that they are lifted by a sale to end all sales on items that, because of the sale, you can now afford. But uplifting in the sense of undergoing an experience with a perceptive force that moves you to the values of beauty, loveliness, aesthetic brilliance, excellence, or acute pleasure. I do not want to say that economic experiences and desires are lower than these other lovely ones. Nor do I want to say that Sam was not excellent at what he did. I do want to say with an initial obviousness that there is a big difference—even a gulf—between the interests and desires that Wal-Mart means and the kind of experience I had that early morning when I was looking at the stars and the image of Wal-Mart came barreling in. And I want to say, too, that there is a factor of indifference that oddly connects them.

The first thing that struck me at that moment of awkward conjunction was the difference in light, the difference with which I began this discussion. In my experience, Wal-Mart presents itself in a glare that continues by metaphor through its insistent, rough, and imposing meanings in our society. A clear night sky, by stark contrast, is vastly dark, and the ethereal darkness *allows* the sidereal lights to shine (as far as human experience goes). When a Wal-Mart and a clear night's sky come together—I ask you to imagine from a growing distance and height, as though you were drawing away from the earth, a shining Wal-Mart complex at night with a backdrop of unclouded sky—the glare of the store overrides the starlight up close. But as you see the store from above and beyond the glare's power, it is distantly, almost indifferently aglow, increasingly starlike as our distance from it grows, decreasing in size, its illuminated parking lot and access streets seeming like small intensities of light scattered from the store, now invested with the serenity that comes with distance. It's not imposing from this distance, and above it, all around for as far as you can see, dark sky in continuity with the distance and filled with stars. Far beyond, the Milky Way.

In my image the store does not appear to be very significant. There is something about the vastness of the sky that, when contemplated, can diminish most appearances, diminish especially the importunateness that might accompany the proximity of forcefully significant things. In the image Wal-Mart's own indifference seems illuminated: In spite of making a lot of differences up close, in a contemplated distance against the starry backdrop it seems so temporary, almost accidental, so unrequired in a big picture. It's just there, and its prospects for the next hundred thousand years don't look good.

Before I address the indifference of this heavenly power in its diminishing of significances in human experience, I note that the word *heavens* has five very distinct suggestions: an expanse of space that seems to arch over the earth; the dwelling place of deities or a deity; a spiritual state of communion with deities or a deity; a place of utmost happiness; an exceptionally harmonious state of mind, usually with divine manifestation. I have in mind the first suggestion—an expanse of space that seems to arch over the earth—with the qualification of a cloudless night on that part of the earth from which the sky is seen: the heavens in a cloudless night. I do not wish to suggest anything about divinity. But I do want to show a certain correlation between a way of seeing things—a certain kind of mentation, an orientation of human spirit—and the appearing of a clear night's sky. My guess is that some of the qualities of this spiritual event have moved people to attach divinity to it so as to anchor it in something that seems more definite than the spiritual event seems to be on its own. While my intention is to speak about and to some extent from such an ethereal mentation, I do not intend to broach a theological or religious terrain.

A dimension of indifference to personal considerations describes competition and is disturbingly obvious in Wal-Mart's appearances.[7] With all of Sam's passion he gave nonetheless to his organization a rare intensity of the indifference that characterizes all competitive enterprises. It's a quasi-ethical indifference defined by bottom lines, an economy of costs, prices, efficiency, and the draw of victory.

---

7. I believe what Sam Walton said about himself and what others said about him: His work and passion were more about winning and dominating than about money as such. Well before he was sixty, he had more money than he could use. And he had no intention of quitting the field until myeloma killed him when he was seventy-two. He quite literally led cheers—was a cheerleader—at meetings of his "associates," and he played "on the field" as captain of his team. He says in his autobiography that no team lost when he was playing on it—his high school team won state championships in football and basketball. And, of course, his "Wal-Mart team" beat all the competition.

A good competitor learns from his opponents, studies them with zest and often with admiration. As far as the competition is concerned, nothing personal is meant. It's simply a matter of trying to win. Nor in most instances is it a personal issue when a player is demoted or moved off the team. There is a wonderfully indifferent objectivity to the bottom line of winning, and those who help most, play. The rules of the game establish what winning and losing are. Laws and practices set perimeters for play— sometimes very flexible perimeters—a range for fudging, and penalties for violations. The means of play—whether it's a ball or money or pawns, knights, and queens—are also defined. And away we go! When we are lucky we can trust our coach and our captain to lead us to the glory of victory. Along the way it's a question of playing well and overwhelming the opponent.

This kind of indifference in competing constitutes a major part of the Wal-Mart phenomenon. It plays a big role in providing the meaning of "big" when the corporation appears big in relation to smaller competitors. In its indifference to persons and their value, Wal-Mart the competitor appears like an inhuman juggernaut rolling over other stores—unfairly rolling over them in the view of many because of the impact of its size. Its enormity magnifies exponentially the appearance of its indifference, while its competitive indifference to other values in turn magnifies its size. There are no divisions of weight. Wal-Mart smashes flyweights and lightweights in small towns, while it beats the heavyweights—K-Mart, Sears, and Target. It is indifferent to the interests of its opponents as long as they have customers who could shop in its stores, and it is largely indifferent to values outside of practical, business endeavor.

One of the requirements for a responsible discount store is to cut every piece of fat from its overhead and to pass the savings on to customers. The company's responsibility is to prices for customers, growth in volume, expansion, and profit. The indifference of that responsibility, in the context of competitive selling, shows Wal-Mart as essentially uncaring for the value of whatever or whoever adds to its overhead and as caring only for what or who helps it to "stomp the comp." This indifference shines through the rhetoric of "one big family" and the down-home image that Sam and his successors tried so hard to maintain. It makes all talk of care—care for employees (i.e., "family associates"), care for communities, care in the form of "Buy America," care for individual customers—seem hollow even when it might be sincerely meant—because the "lights" of Wal-Mart's appearing— its meanings—are so much engendered by the indifference of competing and bottom lines.

When we see Wal-Mart in this light—or any other supermart retailer, for that matter—and put it in the context of the heavens, we see very different kinds of indifference. Sidereal light brings with it no care for Wal-Mart, its responsibility, its goodness or its badness. Nor for whom the store helps or harms. The heavens leave Wal-Mart alone, utterly diminished in its dimensions, as though it were nothing of significance, as though it were without light. The heavens have no competitors. They are without game, players, or human dimension. Wal-Mart's element of indifference glares in competition. The heavens shine forth ethereally with unearthly light in space so other to human dimension that it attracts words like "pure" and "eternal." When we think of "ethereal" we think of intangible delicacy, as though starlight did not touch our eyes, as though it were immaterial and belonged to gods. Such ethereal fire as sidereal light, however, cares absolutely less than Wal-Mart cares and is absolutely more indifferent than Wal-Mart at its competitive best. Wal-Mart, for better or for worse, is an ethical entity, an expression of an ethos. The heavens, in their difference from human appropriation, are not.

Yet, we find the ethereal light of stars beautiful.

This relation of indifference and beauty in human experiences of stars is striking. We are able to cut them down to size by arranging what we see of them in pictorial orders—dippers, dragons, dogs, gods, and warriors. Or we may mix additives into their sight—divinity, nature, or value. But in contemplating them we find with them an inhuman vastness, something quite without solution and quite other to the meanings by which we recognize and name them. We go to Wal-Mart to save money on what we buy or to get something that we cannot afford at other stores. But we go to the stars—mind them, hold ourselves still before them—with an elemental draw as though, in attending them, we were released from care.[8] Is that because of some primordial dynamics? Some response that is outside of our intelligent functions? Something more like a kinship with water than like an ability to make judgments? I don't know. But for whatever reasons of biology or history, the heavens in their lambent indifference with human cares move people and often instill in them a sense of ethereal mystery.

This quality of vast, vast carelessness is, I expect, no less present for those whose business is watching stars, calculating and measuring their spaces, figuring out the kinds of things they are, and thinking about where

---

8. Beauty of this sort did not play a major role in Sam's life, and it does not play much of a role in the lives of many people—people who are suffering terribly, for example, or people who are thoroughly absorbed in some project. In the midst of our cares we do not feel the need for one more careless dimension. In my experience, considerable energy and attention are required for minding the heavens, a certain turn of mind that is very different from a practical mind-set. It's hard to mind the store and the heavens at the same time, although there is room for glancing up on the way to work at 5:30 AM and thinking, Dang, they're pretty.

they came from. Their strangeness, no less today than in the very early times of Babylonians and Egyptians, seems to harbor secrets that only people with special knowledge can understand. People are also strange as they look to the heavens for meanings. It's not strange to look to Wal-Mart for meanings; the organization and its stores are awash in meanings. But the heavens? I expect that if we want to find any meanings there we will first have to import them. The heavens do make a wonderful playground for meaning-importation—at night a big open field of darkness with those uncountable shining, sometimes brilliant, sometimes faint lights, mystery compounded by infinity. People import narratives that "capture," as we might say, a sense of mystery and wonder. Or we count. Or do versions of Rorschach as we see patterns. Or measure and speculate. But with all that, to all appearances the heavens don't care. And yet they appear beautiful to us.

There is not a lot to do when you encounter something that you experience as beautiful, awesome, or ethereal. As far as I can tell, these experiences are ephemeral—they do not last long in their intensity, but they seem so intense and compelling while they last. It's as though something elemental comes and goes in its phenomenal quality and yet also appears to remain in secreted careless presence, something you can't do much about or with, something whose experience has a lot of history but whose presence doesn't even hint at containment within a history. The beautiful aspect appears completely useless—astonishingly useless and beyond the ethos of its engagement, requiring for its appreciation time and attention that are very different from the attention that, say, a store requires.

I think that when the image of my local Wal-Mart intruded on my ethereal reverie, something in my awareness was making a move toward toning down (my)/the celestial engagement. The heavens were vast that dark, early morning. As best as I can remember I wasn't close to (an event of) losing my sense of self or entering into a Satori-like merger with a heavenly All. (Or into a cosmic womb, either.) But as I contemplated the heavens so impractically, I was transported into a vastness of space, darkness, and light that appeared to me (as) wonderfully beautiful and (appeared as) beyond any meaning that I might ascribe to it. So utterly beyond and yet so resonant in my experience. Perhaps the jokester of my psyche did a little number on the fusion taking place in my unworldly mind. Perhaps some aspect of my spirit, in anxiety before this intangible threat to earthly practicality, fled to the most mundane thing he could think of at the moment. Perhaps the spirit of American, competitive inventiveness rose up in offense before the force of this beauty without use, face, or meaning and beyond the ascriptions of interpreters. Or perhaps the jokester came with the heavens and put Wal-Mart and its extraordinary, if indifferent, expression of many

American values into the appearance of the starry heavens, put Wal-Mart and those values there as though they formed a constellation, translating them and all that they mean into the rarified element of darkness, space, and starlight, allowing them to appear with beauty, their glare of store-light destroyed. Perhaps the jokester put them in the heavens to shine with the indifference of sidereal bodies as their meanings faded in starlight.

I can say retrospectively that there was something beautiful about Wal-Mart in that moment, although I hardly noticed it in the shock of its arrival. It shone without glare in its translation. In that appearance there was nothing of care or value. Certainly no competitiveness. It was just there in an element of indifference that it could not own or trade; it was taken from itself and remaindered in a beautiful event of con-fusion that didn't last very long.

In that brief moment shone Wal-Mart's momentary necessity, its constellation-like presence, removed from its day-to-day-force, its "plunk" quality as in "plunk, there it is." It showed that quality of indifference that you can experience if you simply contemplate its phenomenon or one of its boxy supermarts—the kind of indifference that makes it available for pop art, for exemplarity of aspects of our culture, or, strangely enough, for amazed contemplation in the face of its existence. Wal-Mart seems to be outlined by the definitive indifference of the accidental cultural aspects of Sam's life—accidental in the sense that there could be other qualities, but definitive in the sense that that's the way it was. That was the thing, as he might have said. Wal-Mart is defined also by a history of practices that make business success likely in our society. And it is defined in part by the indifferent differences between it and the heavens. Such things as these have no care. They simply define the thing, indifferent to whatever happens.

When it comes to the heavens, there is something fitting about the impractical, ethereal state of mind that contemplates them. I can say from firsthand experience that if you are an ambitious retailer you do not want someone much given to ethereal contemplation on your management team. Such a person can do mindless work, like washing the windows or stocking the shelves. But when retailers need someone who turns his mind fully and with dedicated excitement to the extremely careful work of making a profit at a store, they do not want a person who gets by practically at a minimum and dreams dreams, humming perhaps, while making space for a new load of socks. On the other hand, when the thing is to contemplate—or even just to see—ethereal beauties, it's the impractical mind that you want. Some people are spiritually gifted and can actually manage things with enthusiasm and then shift into a contemplative disposition. But in any case, for something beautiful to inhabit our lives, we need a certain kind of energy and noticing, and usually a glance won't do. To attend to what is without practicality and use, something that doesn't pay and can't be paid, something without political import, something ethereally present (something like the stars or Wal-Mart's constellation aspect), people have to release themselves for a time from the force of ethical obligation, care-filled involvements, and seriousness about themselves. Such events need spiritual transfixing. The indifference of the heavens seems to require this intense, attentive indifference of mind. The way we interpret such events is, of course, a matter considerably different from those events. Interpretation is indeed ethical and political action. But the event in which something lovely and careless appears is one in which people and their cares are diminished. In attentiveness to such events, people go with the diminishment and, for a time at least, allow their attention to be held in the event by the event. Transfixion. A person can fall in love that way. And/or a person can be frightened. Escape and offense, too, as well as absorption are options that are never far from attended happenings of ethereal beauty. But usually, I believe, such events aren't all that dramatic. They simply require a particular kind of predisposition that is otherwise fairly useless, one that allows people to enter into a conjunction with the heavens (or whatever else is beautiful), to forget for a time nearly everything else, and perhaps to return to something elemental and usually hidden—that mind-set and its resonance do not create stores, demolish opponents, seek to dominate, or even to find converts to contemplation. They are fused with indifferent phenomena and are thus indifferent to such endeavors. I have no intention of suggesting that an ethics or a politics should be based on such reverie. But I do think that its indifferent view brings home something neither human nor divine, adds something of beauty to lives that take the time and have the mind for it, and brings with it an attentiveness that is missing in Wal-Mart's day-to-day glare—and missing also from most of the other rhythms of human endeavor that Wal-Mart makes evident in our lives.

I went to the Atherton Street Wal-Mart, of course, not long after my reverie and return to State College. It's open twenty-four hours a day, seven days a week, so if you work at night you can drop in at midnight and pick up milk or Coke or crackers to supplement your "lunch," drive over at 2:00 AM if you need aspirin or Oragel, or stop by after work at 5:00 AM and get a thermos for your daughter's lunch box before she goes to school. I was greeted and offered a shopping cart by an elderly gentleman whom the store hired to watch for "slippage," that is, shoplifting, as well as for greeting. (He receives much lower wages than a police officer would receive and performs two duties at once, thus holding down overhead.) I blinked in the fluorescence, looked over the vast array of shelves and goods that stretched out before me, and recalled its constellation as I experienced it a few weeks earlier. No constellation here. I needed a new rake and wanted to get film developed, and returned before midday. At this time of the morning, 9:00 AM, coffee and Coke drinkers were in the café, many with ball caps on their gray hair. The computer department was in business, and the return counter had a short line of customers with goods under their arms and children in tow. People moved all around with carts. There were new displays of candy, juice, and chips with signs showing exceptionally low prices—the lead items that would draw people in so they would also buy other things with a higher markup. Business as usual.

For a moment I tried to imagine more vividly the store in the heavens. The best I could do was to recall *that* it had appeared among the stars. But I felt, as usual, its strange mix of competitive indifference and practical concern in its reflection of us consumers, its sense of carefully and indifferently buying and selling. I knew also that it lives in a context of overarching indifferences vastly greater than its own superstore dimensions. And I knew that it is no threat to experiences of beauty, no matter how unbeautiful it is, that its indifference as it appalls us is less distant from sidereal splendor than a glance would tell us, that its glaring light, like our lives, brings home, however awkwardly, a distance that beauty is made of.

I hope that you can see that I have been thinking of Wal-Mart's *appearance* by reference to its violation of important values in our culture, its reflection of aspects of the society that allows it to thrive, and its embodiment of values that many of us in this society affirm. I wanted to show that no aspects of its appearing and none of the values that appear define the occurrence of its appearing. The appearing of Wal-Mart seems to be indifferent to the multiple, often-opposed differentials that make up its social identity. From this angle of view Wal-Mart's indifference to many humane values in our culture appears strangely coordinate with the occurrence of its appearing.

Further, the appearing of Wal-Mart in my reverie and in our imagining it with the night sky as an active background—such appearing showed a vast indifference to Wal-Mart's existence and life. Its own indifference to some values that many of us find important for human living is trumped by celestial indifference.

In the reverie I noted, for example, Wal-Mart shines in a way that releases it from its meaning and from the meanings of our judgments that condemn it or appreciate it. In this indifference we can find something of beauty in Wal-Mart's appearance, something surprising that can lift people's spirits from the circumscription of our ethos. In this release, indifference to ethos appears as a strange friend to human lives. Indifference to lives seems to be part of this strangeness that is part of the draw in beautiful appearances.

There is no chance that Helen's simulacra have revisited the West in the form of Wal-Mart. But very likely there is something deviously in common in her simulacra and Wal-Mart's appearing. It's that distance and indifference that figures the lineage of early Nemesis, the distance and indifference that gives appearing lines and boundaries to disappear and still, in their fading, to shine differently and unreachably. Nemesis's double wisdom counsels: Don't violate the boundaries; let the boundaries go. Destruction follows violation, and serious, if moral, aridity follows those who hold too tightly. Doesn't Nemesis shine through Wal-Mart's appearing? We get what we unknowingly ask for, even when we hold it in pious condemnation, and in Wal-Mart's precinct things appear in a glare that only distance and fading can overcome.

INDEX

CHARLES E. SCOTT is Distinguished Professor of Philosophy and Director of the Vanderbilt University Center for Ethics. His most recent books include *The Lives of Things* (Indiana University Press, 2002), *The Time of Memory* (SUNY, 1999), *On the Advantages and Disadvantages of Ethics and Politics* (Indiana University Press, 1996), and *The Question of Ethics* (Indiana University Press, 1990). He is co-editor of *Companion to Heidegger's Contributions to Philosophy* (Indiana University Press, 2001).